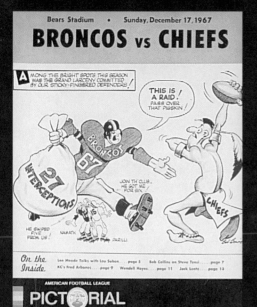

Bears Stadium • Sunday, December 17, 1967

BRONCOS vs CHIEFS

AMONG THE BRIGHT SPOTS THIS SEASON WAS THE GRAND LARCENY COMMITTED BY OUR STICKY-FINGERED DEFENDERS!

THIS IS A RAID! PASS OVER THAT PIGSKIN!

On the Inside

AMERICAN FOOTBALL LEAGUE
PICTORIAL

Price 50 cents

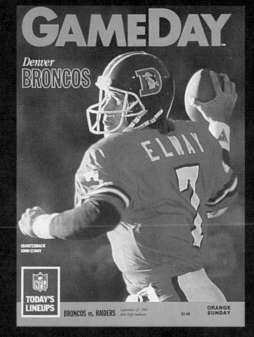

GameDay

Denver BRONCOS

ELWAY 7

QUARTERBACK JOHN ELWAY

NFL TODAY'S LINEUPS

BRONCOS vs. RAIDERS   ORANGE SUNDAY
$2.00

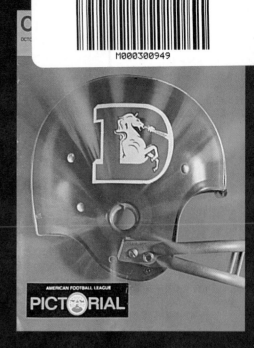

AMERICAN FOOTBALL LEAGUE
PICTORIAL

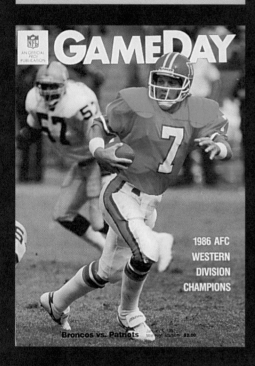

NFL GAMEDAY
AN OFFICIAL PRO! PUBLICATION

1986 AFC WESTERN DIVISION CHAMPIONS

Broncos vs. Patriots $2.00

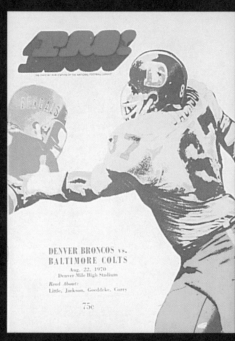

DENVER BRONCOS vs.
BALTIMORE COLTS
Aug. 22, 1970
Denver Mile High Stadium
Read About:
Little, Jackson, Goeddeke, Curry

75¢

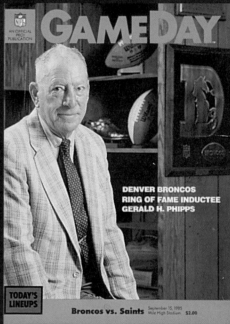

AN OFFICIAL PRO! PUBLICATION

GameDay

DENVER BRONCOS
RING OF FAME INDUCTEE
GERALD H. PHIPPS

TODAY'S LINEUPS

Broncos vs. Saints   September 15, 1985
Mile High Stadium $2.00

pro!

A Doctor in the House

Denver Quarterback Charley Johnson Answers the Call

BRONCOS vs. Steelers

Denver Mile High Stadium
September 22, 1974
$1.00

DENVER BRONCOS

GameDay

NFL

FAN APPRECIATION DAY

BRONCOS vs. STEELERS

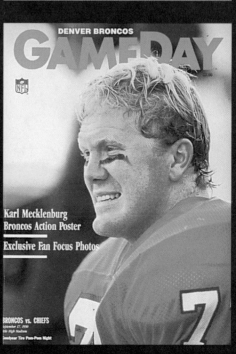

DENVER BRONCOS

GameDay

NFL

Karl Mecklenburg
Broncos Action Poster

Exclusive Fan Focus Photos

BRONCOS vs. CHIEFS
September 17, 1990
Mile High Stadium
Goodyear Tire Pom-Pom Night

WORLD CHAMPION

BRONCOS

OFFICIAL BRONCOS
COLLECTOR'S EDITION

Rich Clarkson

CONTENTS

Andrews McMeel Publishing

an Andrews McMeel Universal company

A RICH CLARKSON BOOK

NOW TAKING ITS PLACE

IN THE PAUL D. BOWLEN

BRONCOS MEMORIAL

CENTRE, THE LONG-

SOUGHT SUPER BOWL

TROPHY

STAFF FOR THIS BOOK
EDITOR: Rich Clarkson
ART DIRECTOR: Carrie Jordan
PRODUCTION COORDINATOR:
Emmett Jordan
EDITORIAL ASSISTANTS: David
Gonzales, Ryan McKee
FOR THE BRONCOS: Sara Gilbertson,
Jim Saccomano, Steve Harbula, Paul
Kirk, Richard Stewart

ISBN:08362-6984-5

LIBRARY OF CONGRESS CATALOGING-IN-
PUBLICATION DATA ON FILE

Rich Clarkson

By Bob Howsom

Where has the time gone? It seems like only yesterday that I received a phone call from Lamar Hunt of the famous Texas Hunts—in fact, it was 40 years ago—that would forever change the sports scene in Denver. Lamar wanted to know if my family would like to get involved in a new football league to compete with the NFL.

Five words altered my life—and many other lives—when I said, "We would have an interest."

We were baseball people at the time. In 1948, my dad, Lee, my brother, Earl, and I bought the minor league team in Denver, the Bears of the six-team Class A Western League. We then purchased a dump site from the city of Denver for $32,000 and began work on Bears Stadium. The 10,000-seat facility opened Aug. 14, 1948. Subsequently, Bears Stadium became Denver Mile High Stadium—home of the Denver Broncos.

In 1965, my dad and I sold our shares in the team to Gerry and Alan Phipps and others. We didn't want to sell but we had become financially overextended in building the South Stands. Nobody needed to pass the hat for the Howsams. However, we definitely were not in the same financial league with people like Lamar, Bud Adams and Baron Hilton.

We could have made a lot more money by selling the team to outsiders but we wanted to keep the Broncos in Denver. The fans of Denver had shown us great loyalty and we wanted to remain loyal to them.

So that's how it happened. The Denver Broncos became charter members of the American Football League in 1960, joined the NFL in 1966, and won the Super Bowl in 1998.

Do I have any regrets about selling the Broncos? None whatsoever. Football was mighty good to me and my family.

And so was baseball. After all, I went on to become the president and general manager of the Cincinnati Reds. We won back-to-back World Series in 1975 and 1976 and played in two others.

I want to give my own Mile High Salute to the fans, John Elway and the other players, Mike Shanahan and his coaching staff and the owner, Pat Bowlen, for winning the Super Bowl.

You have reached the pinnacle of the football world and nobody is more delighted than I am.

Bob Howsam, dean of professional baseball and football in Denver, has homes in Sun City, Ariz., and in Glenwood Springs, Colorado. His wife, Janet, is the daughter of the late Ed Johnson, former Colorado governor and U.S. Senator.

Eric Lars Bakke

WHAT SO PROUDLY WE HAILED

With Bombs Bursting in Air, Super Bowl XXXII began in San Diego's Qualcomm Stadium as 69,912 saluted America's annual sports classic.

By Douglas S. Looney

Rich Clarkson

The Broncos' gallop to the National Football League's pinnacle was a straight line up. There were no stumbles, nobody bucked off, the stirrups never were lost, nobody ever spit the bit; there were no errors in judgement; there was no consternation or second-guessing.

It was a fairy tale of smoothness with nary a setback. Just saddle the willing steed, sit tall and canter to success as the cheers rained down across the Rocky Mountains and far beyond.

That's all there was to it.

Oh, baloney.

Of course exactly the opposite is true. Through the years dating to 1959 when Bob Howsam thought it would be nifty to have professional football in Denver, there had been disappointment and discouragement and dismay. Stunning though it may seem, there were even nay-saying newspaper columns. There was even grousing on the radio talk shows. Hard to believe. However, the clippings and tapes are locked in the little-known Denver Broncos Enemies Vault as evidence.

And that's what makes the ultimate success—that splendiferous first-ever Super Bowl win, 31-24 over the Green Bay Packers on Jan. 25, 1998, that began in the dazzling sunshine of San Diego and ended in the exhilarating glowing lights on the shores of the Pacific Ocean—a moment that will live in millions of hearts and souls forevermore.

If getting to the top is too easy, then planting the flag isn't much fun.

Viva la Broncos. Getting to the top

was numbing in its setbacks. That's why planting the flag atop Mt. Super Bowl in early 1998 was an event of unspeakable glories.

Sunday, Jan. 25, 1998. There are those moribund beings for whom this was just another day. We know different. Of course, the truth is it was a day that dawned in dread—yes, it did, too; let's be honest—for Bronco devotees everywhere. Properly so.

Consider that in four previous trips to the Super Bowl, the Broncos not only lost but–sorry, Pat Bowlen–looked substantially worse than dreadful in the process. Living in infamy: 42-10 to Washington in 1988; 55-10 to San Francisco in 1990. The cold, hard, brutal facts are that in those four attempts, Denver never threatened to win. In each of the four nightmares, the only major success of each day for the players was getting their helmets on frontward.

Consider, too, that the Broncos had no reason to swagger into San Diego and start popping off about being the new sheriff in town. Shoot, they were second to Kansas City in the AFC West. In back-to-back weeks in

December, they lost to Pittsburgh and San Francisco and were just 3-3 in their last six regular-season games. So it was that the Broncos limped—sorry, Pat Bowlen—into the playoffs as a wild card. Only once in NFL history had a wild card team ever won the Super Bowl, the Raiders in 1980. Besides, an AFC team hadn't won the NFL title since 1983. A year that started with so much optimism and success for the Broncos (six straight wins) was teetering at cliff's edge.

There was not a lot for the Broncos and their fans to be puffed up about.

Worse, it was becoming clear to all who would see: John Elway would never win a Super Bowl.

Yup, just like his quarterback buddies in that storied—overhyped?—Class of 1983 who were good but not good enough. Jim Kelly. Dan Marino. Todd Blackledge. All ringless. All were going to be reduced to playing golf as old men and talking about what might have been. Pity.

Finally, consider that while there certainly have been some excellent Bronco performances over the years—any of you happen to remember The

Drive against Cleveland? —the words Denver and Dynasty never appeared linked to one another. However, Denver and Debacle did. For example, the '90s in many ways had not been kind. It opened with the Dan Reeves–led Broncos going 5-11 in 1990. More troubling was that as recently as 1994—that's just three seasons ago for all those of you caught without your abacus—Denver was 7-9 and fourth in the five-team AFC West. That was when Wade Phillips took up a new address. In 1995, the Ponies were fourth again in their division.

Sadly, the 1997 Broncos, for whom hopes were treetop high were more resembling scrub pine as the final regular-season weeks lurched by. They were not looking like the 1927 Yankees. Rather, they were more looking like the every year Cubs.

Yet, through it all, the good times and the bad times and the in-between times, Bronco fans were not dissuaded. Okay, occasionally they would boo but they weren't dissuaded. For 28 years, Mile High Stadium has been sold out. Other teams hate to play here, first because of the passion and zeal of the fans. Second, visitors fret about the altitude, far more psychological than real, but let's keep that part a secret. And third, coming to Denver is hard because while the Broncos previously had been unable to grab the sport's brass ring, they had at times been contenders for it. Alas, their reach exceeded their grasp for the team's entire history. Typically, however, even if Denver wasn't especially strong, somehow the players got pumped up enough to perform well enough to win in Mile High. Dating to 1974, Denver has the best home record in the NFL.

Against this backdrop of dreams gone awry, somehow, some way, the Broncos righted themselves at the perfect moment in 1997–98: Playoff Time.

They dusted Jacksonville, Kansas City, Pittsburgh and You Know Who.

Glory be, hallelujah, raise your arms and lift your voices.

But how did it happen?

1. Last name **ELWAY**, first name John. Is everybody keeping up?

Clearly, without the acquisition of Elway from Baltimore in 1983, things would have been different, shall we say. It was a long time ago, but remember that it wasn't that John specifically wanted to play in Denver. Rather, he wanted to play anywhere except Baltimore. Then-Bronco owner Edgar F. Kaiser Jr. sensed potential value there and presided over the checkbook. He used indelible ink.

The Elway numbers are sensational in their breadth and incomprehensible in their depth. He has won more games than any other NFL quarterback ever; he has led Denver to 45 game-winning fourth-quarter scoring drives; he has thrown and completed more passes for more yards than all 18 of the Hall of Fame quarterbacks; he owns or shares 54 Bronco records. On and on and on and on and on and on and . . .

Is he the best NFL QB ever? Depends who's talking. It is correct that he trails Marino in several categories, including completions and yardage. The analysis of this is simple: Phooey. Look who has a Super Bowl ring and look who doesn't. Case dismissed.

Yet, it may not be the scintillating numbers that best define Elway but rather who he is. Almost always, he has been the steady captain, never too high with victory or too low in defeat. He has engaged in no ugly contractual disputes and, in fact, has cooperated with management in contract restructuring for the greater good. His name has not hit the papers for DUI or spousal abuse or questionable behavior in public parks or fraud

at his car dealerships. His college degree from Stanford adds to his allure. And he has been amazingly durable, starting more games than any Bronco in history.

Too, fans sometimes don't realize how difficult it is being John Elway. He cannot set foot in public without being the focus of fanatical attention. He can't go buy toothpaste at the drugstore in anonymity like us. Truth is, it's exhausting being John Elway. He plays the role spectacularly.

Now, he has not been perfect at every turn. Occasionally, for example, he got to thinking that in addition to being quarterback, he also was owner and coach. But these miscalculations didn't last long. He quickly concluded that player was his strongest position. Regardless, he will do until perfect comes along. Don't hold your breath waiting for someone better.

2. **PAT BOWLEN**.

A discussion of owners is always tricky. If they don't spend money and lose, they are perceived as cheap and stupid. If they spend money and still lose, they are perceived simply as stupid. If they spend and win, the thinking is that anyone can do anything if

For owner Pat Bowlen, the prize at last.

Cornerback Tim McKyer in celebration.

they have enough money. Therefore, it is inordinately difficult for an owner to get it just right. The perfect scenario for an owner would be to spend no money and win. Sure. That will happen when the ocean wears rubber pants to keep its bottom dry.

What Bowlen has done since taking control in 1984 is to be highly involved but not threateningly intrusive. He, like Elway, has been generally calm, focused, steadfast. Bowlen, by all accounts, is not among the elite in the NFL when it comes to personal wealth. Yet, he's hardly a pauper, either. So his attitude has been to spend properly and prudently. It's not a foolish approach.

When Bowlen stares down at his checkbook, he knows some of the dollars will be beautifully spent and others totally misdirected. Already the choice of Kutztown linebacker John Mobley in 1996 is being hailed as genius. But then there was, whoops, the No. 1 pick in 1988 of Syracuse nose tackle Ted Gregory. In 1989, the Broncos selected Arkansas defensive back Steve Atwater first and he has been a star of starry proportion. But then there was, whoops, the No. 1 pick in 1992 of UCLA quarterback Tommy Maddox.

Sometimes, Bowlen can be positively prophetic. Prior to last year's Super Bowl season, he said, "I want to be number one in everything."

3. COACH MIKE SHANAHAN.

Every coach ever selected is a crapshoot. Truth be uttered, nobody knew or even suspected how good Bear Bryant would be or Vince Lombardi or Tom Osborne or Joe Paterno or Paul Brown or George Halas. And so it was with Shanahan.

After three seasons as Bronco boss, Shanahan has answered all questions. What he had to do when Bowlen signed him up was three things: Get along with Bowlen, get along with Elway, win games. Life is very simple. Shanahan devoted himself to these principles. It worked.

As a former Bronco and 49er assistant, he developed a deserved reputation as an offensive mastermind. Proof: In 1997, the Broncos scored 583 points, fifth most in NFL history.

Too, timing is everything and so it was with Shanahan. He had a brief tenure in 1988–89 as head coach of the then L.A. Raiders. Many blame Shanahan's troubles on Raider owner Al Davis. Yet, the larger truth is Shanahan was simply a few years too young and inexperienced for that fishbowl and that man. But when he came to Denver in 1995, he was 41 years old, all buffed up and ready for the NFL coaching rigors.

4. THE BRONCOS HAVE BEEN VERY, VERY FORTUNATE IN THE DRAFT.

Time for another hard truth: Luck may count equally with talent. Tyrone Braxton, who has been an able and talented mainstay at safety, was a 12th-round pick in 1987. Translation: Nobody thought he'd play in the NFL. Denver took him because war room strategists couldn't think of anybody else. In 1990, tight end Shannon Sharpe was a seventh-rounder. Translation: Real borderline. All

Sharpe has done is be the best tight end in the league since 1990 (465 receptions) and by far the best in 1997. For six straight years, Sharpe has been selected for the Pro Bowl. Center Tom Nalen was a seventh-rounder in 1994. Translation: Ho-hum. He turned into an all-pro.

And then, in 1995, came an unknown Georgia running back with a reputation and body the size of a peanut, Terrell Davis. He was a sixth-rounder, the 196th player chosen. Translation: Might become a useful practice field contributor. My goodness. In three seasons, he has gone to the Pro Bowl twice. He was the Super Bowl MVP. His 495 carries for 2,331 yards in the '97-'98 regular and postseason is the most in NFL history, ahead of Eric Dickerson and Barry Sanders.

All Davis has become is the best running back Denver has ever had. That includes Floyd Little.

5. THE BRONCOS HAVE MADE MYRIAD NOTABLY ASTUTE TRADES AND FREE AGENT ACQUISITIONS.

Here, Denver brass has been thinking especially clearly. They had Elway, who couldn't do it all, as they had fervently hoped. What made sense was providing quality help. And they had better provide it quickly, they reasoned, as all evidence was Elway might not play forever, as they had fervently hoped.

A signal that Bowlen and his group were going seriously gunning for the title came in 1993 when they traded Minnesota for superior left tackle Gary Zimmerman. Elway couldn't stop grinning. Not being leveled so often from his blind side seemed to appeal to John. In '94, the Broncs signed up cornerback Ray Crockett and wide receiver Rod Smith. The next year it was wide receiver Ed McCaffrey and guard

Mark Schlereth. In '96, into Mile High came linebacker Bill Romanowski and defensive end Alfred Williams.

Then, prior to 1997, in a talent hunt of startling dimension, Denver signed 21 new players. Most noteworthy was defensive end Neil Smith.

So is the past prologue? One can only hope.

These hopes received a giant infusion when John Elway announced in late spring that he would return for one more star turn. The enormous sighs emanating from Bronco headquarters produced gale-force winds along the Front Range. Said an elated Pat Bowlen: "I've been waiting and hoping for this moment for a long time."

The will he or won't he drama had Bronco fans at the precipice for four months.

When Elway announced his cataclysmic decision, he was his usual casual, composed, understated self: "Everyone keeps congratulating me for coming back. The thing is, I never left. The bottom line is that I just wasn't ready to quit competing."

And that comment—"I just wasn't ready to quit competing"—goes right past the heart of John Elway to his soul. If ever a player loved to compete for the sake of competing, it's Elway. The delight in winning is worth the pain of losing to him. Strap on the hat, put the ball on the 20 and let's go find out who's best. Hey, it's fun, this pass and catch stuff, this being knocked down and getting back up.

That's the essence of John.

It's a wondrous scenario. Elway returns for 1998 not for the money, not for the adulation, not to establish more records, not because people told him to or told him not to. No, sir. No. 7 is back because competing is just too doggoned much fun to walk away from.

THE SPECIAL POSTGAME

David Gonzales

REJOICING: THE STRATEGIST

AND THE FACILITATOR

Chortles Elway, "It's going to be fun being the world champions."

Shanahan agrees, apparently feeling it's going to be a whole lot more fun being world champs with Elway than without him. Says the coach, whose mother raised no fool, "I think it's a perfect situation."

Fans, of course, are bonkers in delight.

And so the trek up Mt. NFL begins anew, from the bottom, as always. The horses are saddled but the twisty, narrow trail is dangerous. The journey, as always, is fraught with peril and a single misstep can be catastrophic.

But every journey must start with a single you-know-what and this one starts with high spirit and great optimism.

Yet, no matter what the future holds, that blazing moment in San Diego when the Broncos finally won the Super Bowl can never be tarnished nor ever taken away.

Ah, yes, the Broncos know what all of us know. We've all won and we've all lost and winning is a lot more fun.

Douglas S. Looney was a senior writer for Sports Illustrated for more than 21 years. He now is senior sports columnist for the Christian Science Monitor. He lives in Boulder.

THE GAME-CLINCHING TOUCHDOWN—TERRELL DAVIS FOR ONE YARD

THROUGH A MAMMOTH HOLE IN THE GREEN BAY LINE. DID THE PACKERS GIVE

IT AWAY JUST TO GET THE BALL WITH TIME TO SCORE? IF SO, IT WAS THE

MISCALCULATION OF THE GAME: UNDERESTIMATING THE BRONCO'S DEFENSE.

WHILE TERRELL DAVIS DEFINED THE RUNNING GAME, ELWAY'S BULLET

PASSES TO SHANNON SHARPE AND ED McCAFFREY WERE THE SPARKS OF

THE SCORING DRIVES. McCAFFREY CRAFTED A 36-YARD GAIN HERE,

THE LONGEST OF SUPER BOWL XXXII.

David Gonzales

David Gonzales

IN THE KEY PLAY OF THE KEY DRIVE IN THE

FOURTH QUARTER, TERRELL DAVIS SWEPT RIGHT

FOR 17 YARDS TO THE ONE-YARD LINE – AND TO THE

MVP TITLE OF THE GAME. HE SCORED ON THE

NEXT PLAY, BUT THE PACKERS' BRETT FAVRE

(BELOW) WAS NOT SO FORTUNATE: HE HAD JOHN

MOBLEY IN HIS FACE.

David Gonzales

Game
Time

LAS VEGAS

Rich Clarkson

AS THE SPECTACLE OF SUPER BOWL XXXII UNFOLDED, THE BRONCOS

COULD FEEL AT HOME IN THIS STADIUM SO STEEPED IN AFL

HISTORY. WHETHER BEARING THE ORIGINAL NAME OF JACK MURPHY

OR TODAY'S QUALCOMM, IT WAS TO BE THE BRONCO'S TURF THIS DAY

THOSE MOMENTS OF GLORY BEGAN AT MIDFIELD

AND CONTINUED INTO THE NIGHT AND INTO THE

DAYS AFTER. FOR JOHN ELWAY BEING CARRIED

FROM THE FIELD OR NEIL SMITH WHO BEGAN HIS

OWN VICTORY CELEBRATION. PREVIOUS AGONIES

TURNED TO ULTIMATE ECSTASIES.

David Gonzales

David Gonzales

1959

The first organizational meeting of the American Football League was held in Chicago with Bob Howsom, principal owner of the Broncos, named as a charter member along with teams from New York, Dallas, Los Angeles, Minneapolis and Houston.

1960

The first Broncos training camp with head coach Frank Filchock opened at the Colorado School of Mines. After losing all their preseason exhibition games, the Broncos defeated the Boston Patriots 13-10 in history's first AFL game.

1961

Gerald Phipps and Cal Kunz buy out the Howsom brothers. The Broncos' second season features Lionel Taylor setting a professional record with 100 pass receptions for the season.

1962

Jack Faulkner becomes new head coach and general manager and the Broncos' notorious vertically striped socks are banished and burned. The All-AFL team includes Broncos *Eldon Danenhauer,* Lionel Taylor, *Goose Gonsoulin* and Bob Zeman.

1965

With Mac Speedie as head coach, the Broncos become a solid hometown Denver franchise when Gerald and Allan Phipps purchase remaining stock in Empire Sports, the Broncos' holding group. Behind the passing of *Frank Tripuka, Lionel Taylor* makes his 500th pass catch to win his fifth AFL pass receiving crown and Abner Haynes earns the league kickoff return title.

1966

Ray Malavasi is named head coach in September, but is replaced by Lou Saban in December. But the big news is the merger of the AFNFL and the upstart AFL.

1968

Broncos fans raise $1.8 million to build a second deck on Bears Stadium and the facility's name is changed to Denver Mile High Stadium. And the Broncos move into a new headquarters building with adjoining practice field at 5700 Logan St.

1970

Season ticket sales hit an all-time high of 43,584. *Floyd Little* wins the AFC rushing title with 901 yards for the season.

1971

Lou Saban ends a five-year stint as Broncos coach and a search for a new head coach brings Stanford's John Ralston to Denver for the next season. Floyd Little keeps rushing, this year for 1,133 yards and another Broncos record. The season ticket sales reached 47,500, so many that the Broncos stopped sale of tickets as seats ran out.

1973

ABC's Monday Night Football becomes "Orange Monday" and features the Broncos against the Raiders ending in a tie game 23-23 on a 35-yard Jim Turner field goal. The Broncos go on to their first winning season and John Ralston is named AFC Coach of the Year. *Charlie Johnson* becomes the 18th quarterback in pro history to go over 20,000 career yards.

1974

Denver voters approve a $25 million bond issue to expand Mile High Stadium to 75,000 seats and the Broncos respond with another winning season, highlighted by *Otis Armstrong's* single-game rushing mark of 183 yards against the Houston Oilers.

1977

Red Miller replaces John Ralston as head coach and promptly fashions' the Broncos–first Super Bowl–bound team, with impressive regular season wins over the world-champion Raiders and Baltimore Colts. The largest crowd to then watch a sporting event in Colorado, 75,011, watched the Broncos stop the Pittsburgh Steelers 34-21 in the playoffs.

1981

Edgar Kaiser buys the Broncos and names *Dan Reeves* as head coach. Morton sets a team single-season record for yardage gained (3,213) while wide receiver *Steve Watson* leads the AFC in receiving yards and touchdown receptions (13).

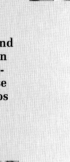

1982

The first regular-season strike in NFL history cancels games for eight weeks. *Rick Upchurch* returns a punt 78 yards against Kansas City to tie the all-time pro football record of eight career touchdowns on punt returns.

1978

The Broncos' first Super Bowl appearance goes awry as the Dallas Cowboys win 27-10. But fan fervor is high — only 143 season ticket holders do not renew their seats and quarterback *Craig Morton* leads the Broncos to the AFC West crown. The eventual Super Bowl champion Pittsburgh Steelers stop the season with a December playoff win.

1983

In the biggest trade in franchise history, the Broncos acquire John Elway from the Baltimore Colts and sign him to a five-year contract. In December, he throws three fourth-quarter touchdown passes to erase a 19-0 deficit and lead the Broncos to a stunning 21-19 win over the same Colts.

1984

Pat Bowlen becomes the new owner and CEO of the Broncos. The team wins a franchise-record 13 regular-season games, but loses to Pittsburgh 24-17 in the divisional playoff game.

1987

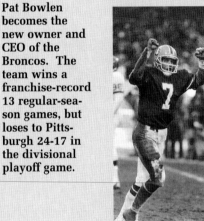

The Broncos go to the Super Bowl as 63,000 fans assemble in Mile High Stadium for a send-off rally. The Broncos lose to the *New York Giants* 39-20 before 101,000 in the Rose Bowl. But everyone remembers how the Broncos got there with a come-from-behind 23-20 win over Cleveland. *The Drive* will go down as one of the most memorable moments in team history.

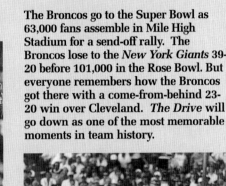

1988

It's the Super Bowl again, this time against the *Washington Redskins* in San Diego's Jack Murphy Stadium and the outcome is not pretty: Washington wins 42-10.

1990

This year's Broncos Super Bowl appearance in the New Orleans Superdome is no more rewarding: Denver loses Super Bowl XXIV to the *San Francisco 49ers* 55-10. The Broncos move into their new Dove Valley headquarters, the Paul D. Bowlen Memorial Center.

1993

Wade Phillips replaces Dan Reeves as coach of the Broncos and season ticket sales assure the team of its 24th consecutive sellout campaign at Mile High Stadium.

1995

Mike Shanahan becomes the 11th coach of the Broncos, returning to Denver from the San Francisco 49ers, who fall to Denver 24-10 in the preseason American Bowl in Tokyo.

1996

Terrell Davis wins the AFC rushing title with 1,538 yards and John Elway becomes the winningest quarterback in NFL history. The season comes to an abrupt end after the first of the year when the expansion Jacksonville Jaguars stun the Broncos and all of Denver with a 30-27 loss.

1997

At Last, The Year. The Broncos face Miami in the American Bowl in Mexico City. New uniforms are controversial when introduced, but quickly accepted by fans who are more interested in the games. And the team steadfastly marches to victory in *Super Bowl XXXII* after the first of the year. This was The Year.

IN THE BEGINNING...

Rich Clarkson

Birthplace of the Broncos: the stately atrium lobby of Denver's famed Brown Palace Hotel.

By Lamar Hunt

You might say the Denver Broncos were born in the lobby of the Brown Palace Hotel. At least, that is where Bob Howsom and I sat down to talk about the concept of the American Football League. I felt that Denver was one of the four cities which could be the nucleus of the new league.

Bob was the owner of the Denver Bears minor league baseball team at the time and was prominent in many Denver sports at the time. I called him to inquire if he was interested in talking about football. He said yes and so it was I came to Denver and we met one evening in the spring of 1959 at the Brown Palace. To this day, I can even remember where we sat in the lobby for our conversation.

I had not previously met Bob, but my recruiting of prospective investors for the American Football League took the form of my contacting the individuals who I had learned had expressed interest in purchasing the Chicago Cardinals and moving them elsewhere. And one of those people was Howsom and his city was Denver.

At this point, I had arranged similar meetings with Bud Adams in Houston, a group in Minneapolis and I planned to support the AFL franchise for Dallas. Three years later, we moved the franchise to Kansas City and it became the Chiefs.

By mid-summer, I felt good about the first four cities and thought we were off to a good start. At that point, I sought out two more cities—New York with Harry Wismer and Los Angeles with Baron Hilton as the owners.

It was late July of 1959 and the AFL was ready to be announced.

The first joint meeting of the prospective owners was August 14-15, 1959, in Chicago. This was the first time any of those people had met each other. A simple organizational agreement was prepared (and signed one week later) and the American Football League was a reality.

The agreement called for each of the owners to pay $25,000 into the league treasury, which was, in effect, the price of the franchise.

Suddenly, there was a lot of interest in the new league and we decided to add two more teams, Buffalo with Ralph Wilson and Boston with Billy Sullivan. Three months later, the Minneapolis group dropped out to join the NFL and we replaced them with the Oakland Raiders in February led by principal owners Chet Soda and Wayne Valley.

The first AFL player draft was held in late November and Dean Griffing, the Broncos first general manager, was one of three GMs (there were only three managers named at the time) who organized and conducted the pooled "blind draw" draft. The top eight players' names were put in a hat and each team began drawing names. Each team was allowed one "territorial" choice, a player from their area who might be familiar and popular with the fans. The Broncos' first choice was Roger LeClerc, a center from Trinity College.

But it was because of those early-day players that the Broncos franchise developed and prospered. Lionel Taylor, Frank Tripucka, Gene Mingo, Bud McFaddin, Hardy Brown, Goose Gonsoulin, names which all Denver fans should revere and treasure. Their contributions made possible the success of the AFL and the Broncos of today.

In 1960, I thought Denver was a city ready for professional football. But not everyone else agreed. George Preston Marshall, owner of the NFL's Washington Redskins, told me, "Denver is your huge mistake. They will never draw 10,000 people for a sporting event in that town."

This was after the first season and I tried to tell him they already had done so, but he wouldn't listen. He insisted that we bet $100 and finally, I had to agree. Soon thereafter, I sent him the "game statement" from our first Texans-Broncos game that showed something like 13,000 paid attendance.

Marshall paid off like a soldier. And I still have a copy of the check.

The rivalry between the Broncos and the Chiefs over the years has become one of the best in football. The Chiefs had the upper hand in the early years, but the Broncos have prevailed over much of the past 15 seasons. I remember well the many games of the last 38 seasons because it has been so very competitive.

In 1963 when we had just moved the Chiefs to Kansas City, one of the most memorable games for us was the first regular-season game in Denver. The game was played in the old Denver University stadium, long since torn down, and it was the largest margin of victory by a Chiefs team over the Broncos—59-7. I think it was the only Broncos-Chiefs game every played at D.U. and I remember that it rained. It was particularly important because Sports Illustrated covered the game as a feature story that week and the AFL was searching for real credibility at the time.

I have many good memories of the Broncos over the years. There was Cal Kunz who headed a group that bought out Bob Howsom and helped assure the continuity of the team in Denver. From that group, Gerry and Allan Phipps were two really fine gentlemen who brought the Broncos to ultimate success.

Then there were the many great Broncos games over the years, and I remember well watching the 1984 Monday night 17-14 victory over Green Bay in the freak early-season snowstorm. And in another Mile High snowstorm, Marcus Allen scored a diving touchdown for the Chiefs that set an NFL record.

All the great John Elway comeback wins over the years are certainly a part of pro football history—and many of those were against the Chiefs. but my favorite was the 1994 Monday night comeback win by Joe Montana—a pass to Willie Davis of the Chiefs with only six or eight seconds left. Elway had just scored on a drive only moments before, and then the Chiefs went the length of the field with no timeouts for the 31-28 win.

To this day, ABC has counted that game as one of the greatest Monday Night Football games ever. You can probably understand why it is a favorite of mine.

Those games in Mile High Stadium with those rabid fans in the South Stands have always been special. It is the only continously used professional football site in the AFC from day one of the first year of the original league in 1960. Only Lambeau Field has been used longer in the NFL.

I did not personally see the game but for those of us from the AFL, we all celebrated the first AFL victory over an NFL team—the Broncos over the Detroit Lions in the preseason of 1967.

And in addition to all the exciting Chiefs-Broncos games I have attended over the years, I had the privilege to attend two AFC Championship Games in Mile High. The first, a 20-17 victory over the Oakland Raiders, put the Broncos in their first Super Bowl and the second was the classic victory over Cleveland when Ernest Byner fumbled the ball on the three-yard line, saving Denver's win.

Of all the rivalries in the early years of the AFL and, today, the NFL, the Chiefs and Broncos is one of the best. These two communities with many similarities and close ties have taken these teams to their hearts with much respect for the other. When Kansas City and Denver play, as many fans as possible get tickets to travel to the other city for the weekend.

The rivalry has been intense but full of friendship. Today, we have the utmost respect for owner Pat Bowlen and general manager John Beake. And as I look back on those early years when we were getting the AFL started, it was obvious to me that Denver would be a good football town. Just like I told George Preston Marshall.

Denver indeed turned out not to be just a good football city. It is a great one.

To all in pro football, a Lombardi trophy really looks good in the trophy case. I'm pleased for the Broncos to have one now.

Lamar Hunt has been present more than once when the Broncos won the AFC championship trophy named for the AFL founder—Lamar Hunt.

Lamar Hunt, the owner of the Kansas City Chiefs, was the founder of the American Football League and the architect of the merger of the AFL and NFL. He is credited with the name of "Super Bowl" for the annual world championship game, the first one of which featured his Chiefs losing to the Green Bay Packers. He lives in Dallas.

Studies in determination, dedication, sometimes boredom and occasional frustration are the close-ups of NFL football. Mirrored in these expressions of the moment is the concentration of men intent on their role in a joint effort, that of Broncos victories. These are just some of the famous faces that waited on the sidelines for their moment on the field. The faces may have changed through the years, but the emotions are the same.

Wide receiver Michael Young (1989-92)

Defensive back Steve Foley (1978-86)

Rod Hanna

Defensive end Lyle Alzado (1971-78)

Wide receiver Vance Johnson (1985-93, 1995)

Wide receiver Rick Upchurch (1975-83)

Tackle Claudie Minor (1974-82)

Tight end Clarence Kay (1984-91)

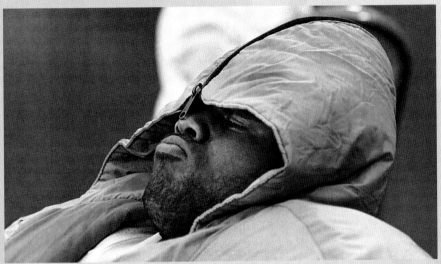

ON THE SIDELINES,

RESOLUTE FACES OF

BRONCOS' DESTINIES

Rod Hanna

Linebacker Randy Gradishar (1975-83)

Kicker Rich Karlis (1982-88)

Rod Hanna

Cornerback Louie Wright (1975-86)

Defensive end Rulon Jones (1980-88)

Rod Hanna

Eric Lars Bakke

Center Keith Bishop (1980, 1982-89)

Defensive end Barney Chavous (1973-85)

Linebacker/defensive end
Karl Mecklenburg (1983-94)

Rod Hanna

Halfback Floyd Little (1967-75)

THE FAMOUS FACES

FROM EARLIER DAYS IN

MILE HIGH STADIUM.

Kicker Jim Turner (1971-79)

Wide receiver Steve Watson (1979-87)

Quarterback Charley Johnson (1972-75)

Denver fans filled the once-expanded Bears Stadium in 1967 and the push was already on for more seats.

In the early years, the Bronco Cheerleaders looked more like the Rockettes.

Broncos spectacle even went to London when the team played the first-ever NFL exhibition game in Great Britain. On that occasion, player Rick Dennison exchanged helmets with a London bobbie.

In the early years, promotions abounded as the new Broncos sought to fill their stadium. Playing first in the Denver University Stadium and then moving to Bears Stadium, since renamed Mile High, ticket sales moved swiftly as Denver embraced the Broncos. The early cheerleaders and the first Thunder mascot added to the spectacle of those games in the 1960s. And at the same time, Denver began adding to Bears Stadium built in 1948 for baseball. In 1959 with the advent of professional football, the south stands and the movable east stands were added to boost the capacity to 34,657 seats. In 1968, a civic drive raised $1.8 million to buy the stadium, giving it to the city and beginning construction of the upper deck that raised the seating to 50,000. The sellout string began in 1970 and in 1974 voters approved a $25 million bond issue to expand the stadium to its current 75,000 Mile High seats.

AS EARLY DAY BRONCOS'

CROWDS GREW, SO TOO

DID THE SPECTACLES

ON THE SIDELINES.

The early day Broncos mascot, Thunder, raced the sidelines after touchdowns.

WHO WILL RIDE *this* DONKEY after the Texans-Broncos Football Game Sunday... a Denver, or a Dallas REALTOR?

Eleven men have coached the Broncos over the 38 years and 96 have served as assistant coaches. Frank Filchock was the first, signed on January 1, 1960, and served for the first two seasons. The longest coaching reign belonged to Dan Reeves, who led the Broncos for 12 seasons. The shortest was Jerry Smith, who finished out the 1971 season when Lou Saban resigned with five games remaining. The winningest coach in Broncos history is current head man Mike Shanahan. Seven of the assistants went on to become NFL head coaches.

Mac Speedie (1964-66)

Lou Saban (1967-71)

Ray Malavasi (1966)

Frank Filchock (1960-61)

Jack Faulkner (1962-64)

Langhead Photographers

28

Rod Hanna

Red Miller (1977-80)

John Ralston (1972-76)

Jerry Smith (1971)

ELEVEN HEAD

COACHES LED

THE BRONCOS

OVER 38 YEARS

Dan Reeves (1981-92) and Wade Phillips (1993-94)

The Colorado School of Mines, nestled against the foothills just out-side Golden, was the first training camp of the Broncos in 1960. It served as their summer home for four different years. The Broncos moved to Colorado State University twice for stints of three and five years and for another three-year term trained at California Poly Pomona. Since 1982, they have taken up home at the University of Northern Colorado in Greeley where the business of preparing for the season, breaking in the rookies and generally doing the uninspiring but necessary toughening takes place.

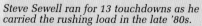
Steve Sewell ran for 13 touchdowns as he carried the rushing load in the late '80s.

The early years' summer camps were at the Colorado School of Mines at Golden where the newly-arrived Cookie Gilchrist admired the view.

Kickoff returns in the hands of Charlie Mitchell in the mid-'60s were under control when he ran back 37 returns for 954 yards in one season.

Rich Clarkson

The training camp site was Colorado State University in the early '60s.

Rod Hanna

Joe Collier had the longest tenure of any Broncos assistant, 19 years culminating in his directing the defense during the Dan Reeves years.

Living in the Rockies means dealing with snow, and over the years Broncos games have seen their fair share. Perhaps no snow game is more memorable than a Monday night matchup with the Packers in 1984, when a freak early October storm produced near-blizzard conditions. A nation of television viewers sat intrigued as stadium workers tried to keep the yard lines clear. But there was no keeping up with the snowstorm. Denver won 17-14 in a game that could hardly be seen by the fourth quarter. But the real victory occurred the next day. The phones at Colorado's ski areas rang out the largest single-day bookings ever.

ON MONDAY NIGHT TELEVISION, THE NATION WATCHED THE BRONCOS BATTLE BOTH GREEN BAY AND A RAGING BLIZZARD.

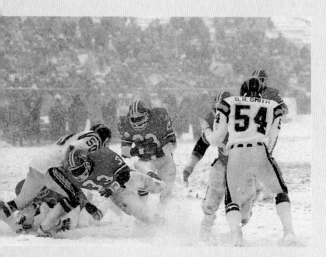

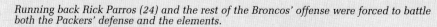

Visibility goes down as the snowfall increases with fans in the stadium often able to see little more than were they in front of their television sets.

Despite the Monday night blizzard, Rich Karlis' bare foot was still able to provide the winning points in Denver's 17-14 victory over Green Bay.

Running back Rick Parros (24) and the rest of the Broncos' offense were forced to battle both the Packers' defense and the elements.

Dan Reeves often had to content with two opponents.

A little of the white stuff couldn't keep 62,546 Broncomaniacs from enjoying 1984's Monday night clash with the Packers.

Footing becomes nearly impossible and grounds crews struggle to first brush away, later shovel away the accumulating snow.

The offense gets the headlines, and the Broncos roster is rich with headline-grabbers. Before Terrell Davis carried the ball, there was Sammy Winder, Otis Armstrong and Floyd Little. Before Shannon Sharpe was catching passes, there was Vance Johnson, Haven Moses and Lionel Taylor. And before Coloradans had ever heard the name Elway, Craig Morton, Charley Johnson and Frank Tripucka led the troops. Kicker Jim Turner contributed 1,423 points over a career which earned him a place in the Broncos Ring of Fame. The entire offense has an amazing franchise record that includes some 90 100-yard rushing games, more than 160 100-yard receiving games and 56 300-yard passing games.

Tight end Clarence Kay's sure hands helped the Broncos defeat the Oilers 34-10 in a 1987 divisional playoff game.

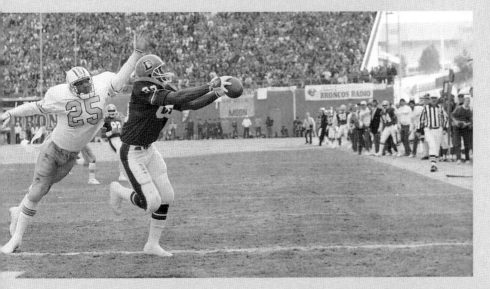

Quarterback Craig Morton earned AFC Most Valuable Player honors in 1977 in leading the Broncos to their first Super Bowl berth.

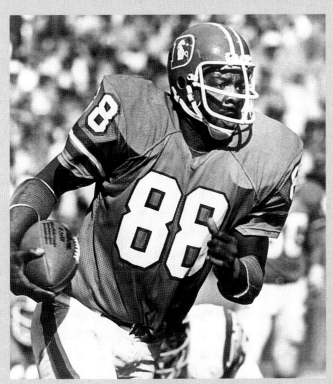

"The Franchise"—(above) running back Floyd Little—was the first No. 1 draft pick ever signed by the Broncos. Tight end Riley Odoms (left) ranks fourth in the Broncos all-time receiving list.

Sammy Winder (left) was the Broncos' main threat at running back from 1982 through 1990. His 5,428 career rushing yards rank him second all-time in team history.

Defense has always been a Denver trademark, even when the "Orange Crush" was just another soda. Warriors like Rich Jackson, Paul Smith and Austin "Goose" Gonsoulin paved the way for the heroics of Randy Gradishar, Louis Wright, Billy Thompson and Tom Jackson, while men like Simon Fletcher, Dennis Smith and Karl Mecklenburg helped the Broncos return to glory in the late 1980s. Of the many Broncos who have appeared in the Pro Bowl, the most appearances have been by the defenders. With that rich tradition, the 1997 season effort placed the Broncos defense No. 1 in the AFC. Defense is a Broncos trademark.

Rod Hanna

Original Ring of Fame inductee Ausin "Goose" Gonsoulin was the all-time AFL leader in interceptions at the end of his Broncos career.

Defensive end Rich Jackson brings down San Diego Chargers quarterback John Hadl and became one of the original four Broncos inducted into the Ring of Fame.

Billy Thompson is regarded by many as the best defensive back in Broncos annals.

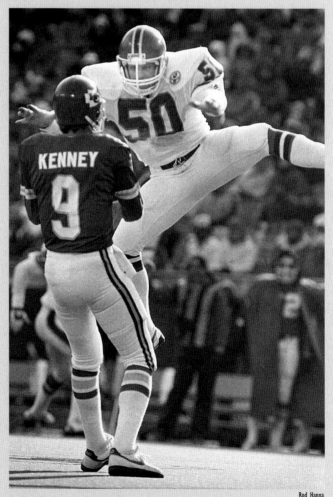

Rod Hanna

Linebacker Jim Ryan arrived at high altitude as Kansas City quarterback Bill Kenney reappraised his intent to pass.

LINEBACKER TOM JACKSON LED THE FAMED "ORANGE CRUSH" DEFENSE FROM 1973-1986.

Four trips to Super Bowls before 1998—and four frustrations followed the euphoria of playing in the biggest game of the season. The Louisana Superdome, the Rose Bowl and Jack Murphy Stadium were all the sites of great anticipation which melted into second-half disappointment. Facing the likes of Joe Montana, Doug Williams, Phil Simms and Roger Staubach, the Broncos struggled without ever gaining control of the game. Yet in each of those years, the Broncos got to the game of the year with thrilling playoff games and seasons of great accomplishment. But without the final reward.

The legandary creator of the National Football League as it evolved, the late Pete Rozelle greeted Broncos players and coaches at the 1987 Super Bowl.

Media day precedes each Super Bowl when hundred of sportswriters and sportscasters record every word.

Rod Hanna (3)

Rich Clarkson

The hoopla before the game has been a part of every Super Bowl, including such spectacles as oversized helmets at the 1989 game as coach Dan Reeves and the Broncos took the field.

Denver fans have cheered their teams on through the championship games, here at Pasadena in 1986.

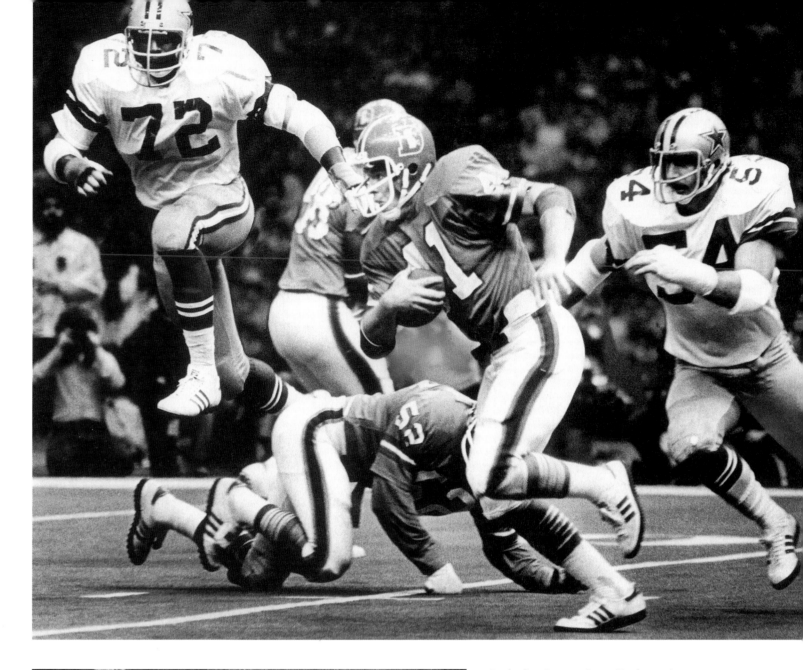

In the first Broncos Super Bowl, running back Rob Lytle (41) scampered around center Mike Montier (52) as the Cowboys' Ed "Too Tall" Jones (72) closed in for the tackle. After the game, Cowboys coach Tom Landry stopped Broncos quarterback Craig Morton for a few consoling words after the 27-10 loss.

NEW ORLEANS IN 1977:

THE COWBOYS

ROPED THE BRONCOS

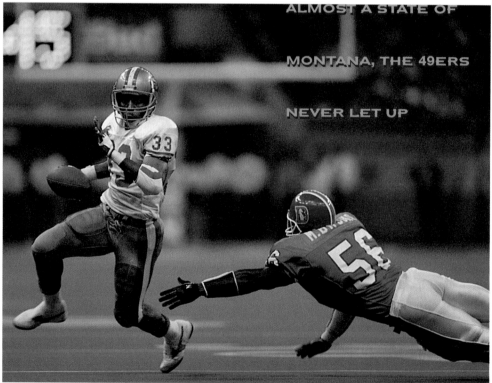

ALMOST A STATE OF

MONTANA, THE 49ERS

NEVER LET UP

Though the faithful traveled to New Orleans, San Diego and Pasadena for Super Bowls in the '80s, the results were similar. Joe Montana led the 49ers to the most one-sided of the lot, 55-10 as the game was quickly out of reach.

Eric Lars Bakke (3)

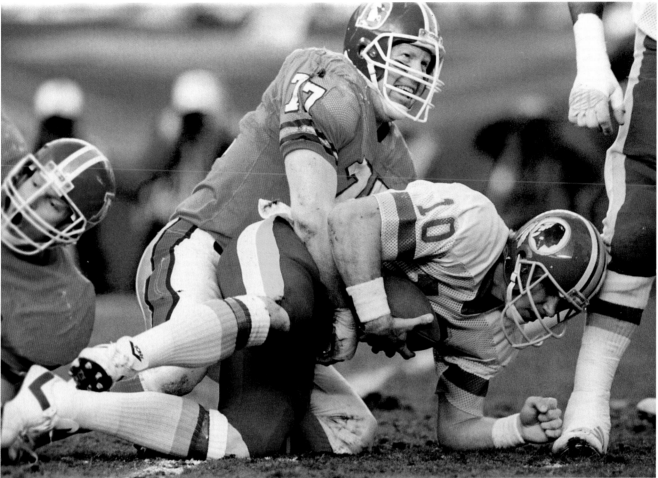

In the 1988 game, Karl Mecklenburg took down Redskins backup quarterback Jay Schroeder, but the expression on Mecklenburg's face shows the game was already decided.

Elway himself was taken down often as the Broncos scrambled with the Redskins in 1987. Fullback Gene Lang (33) found a hole early as the Broncos took a 10-0 lead. But the second quarter began the Redskins deluge that eventually amounted to 42 unanswered points.

John Elway accounted for more than 300 yards against each the Redskins and Giants, often under pressure in games that got away in the second quarter.

Dan Reeves was tight-lipped along with Broncos fans everywhere.

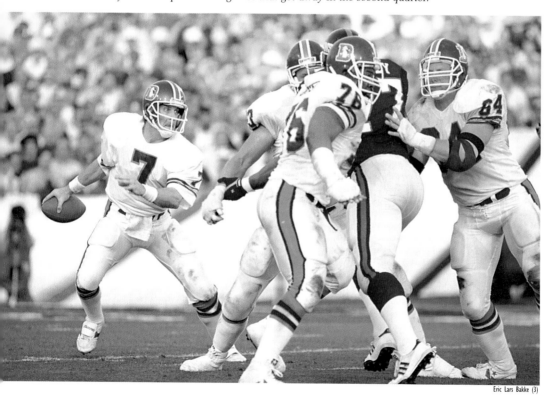

THE PREMIER

QUARTERBACK WITH

NO PLACE TO GO

Faces told the story of those first four Super Bowls. Greg Kragen grimaced.

Sammy Winder watched quietly.

Cornerback Mike Harden couldn't watch.

Defensive end Andre Townsend was open-mouthed.

John Elway was always something more than a great college player whose Stanford days followed a much-watched prep career at Granada Hills High School. It was a sports family with father Jack coaching at Cal State Northridge and later at San Jose State and Stanford. Both a football and baseball player for the Cardinal, he was a consensus All-American and was drafted No. 1 in 1983 as the most publicised college prospect since Joe Namath. Baltimore got him but subsequently traded him to the Broncos amid controversy over the deal. This was the youthful face that arrived in Denver, with high expectations and constant attention.

Although the premier draft choice his senior year, Elway's Stanford days were typically collegiate, complete with a small dormitory room, a water bed and a 12-inch television set.

The high school Elway was an All-American football player his senior year, 1979, as well as an exceptional baseball prospect signed by the Kansas City Royals. He opted for Stanford instead.

Granada Hills retired his jersey but the whole Elway family was as All-American as the proverbial apple pie.

RIFLE PASSES

SET SCHOOL

AND CONFERENCE

RECORDS.

Rich Clarkson (7)

Down the highway at San Jose State, father Jack guided the Spartans' football fotunes.

In college, Elway completed 62 percent of his career passes for 9,349 yards and 77 touchdowns while setting an NCAA record for fewest interceptions, 3.13 percent.

If expectations and attention were not high enough at Elway's first summer camp at the University of Northern Colorado and if there wasn't enough for a rookie quarterback to learn, Denver's media covered him like a blanket. The daily feature was called "The Elway Watch" and his every move and pronouncement was documented—and then dissected.

Training camp began with much to learn. As coach Dan Reeves presided, the other quarterback, Steve DeBerg, went over plays on the blackboard as Elway listened. For that first season, the quarterback coach was veteran former San Diego quarterback John Hadl, who worked with Elway continously.

Rich Clarkson (4)

The training table at the University of Northern Colorado was one of the few times for Elway to relax out of the limelight as one of the ball boys enjoyed ice cream with his new hero.

WRITERS AND BROAD-

CASTERS ALL WANTED

INTERVIEWS AS

"THE ELWAY WATCH"

MARCHED ONWARD.

THE CURTAIN RISES

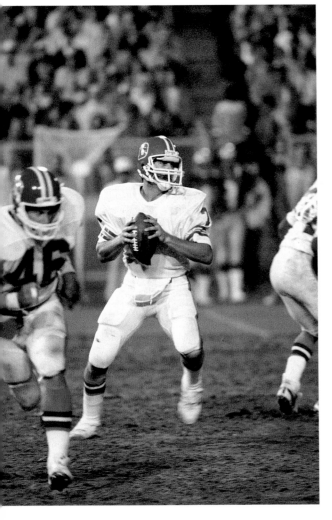

Before the game, Steve DeBerg gave the starting Elway more tips and reassurance in the locker room. On the field, the roaring crowd watched his every move.

AND THE ELWAY

ERA BEGINS

Elway's first start was in pre-season against the Seattle Seahawks and the sold-out Mile High Stadium assembled for the premiere of the hoped-for salvation of the beloved Broncos. He was already the super-star of the moment as well as the future of the team. It was the beginning of a time when hope began turning into eventual reality.

The adulation of kids was already there, even those so fortunate to be ball boys (Chip Beake here) as they watched Elway deliver his first victory along with the promise of good days to come. Denver had its new hero.

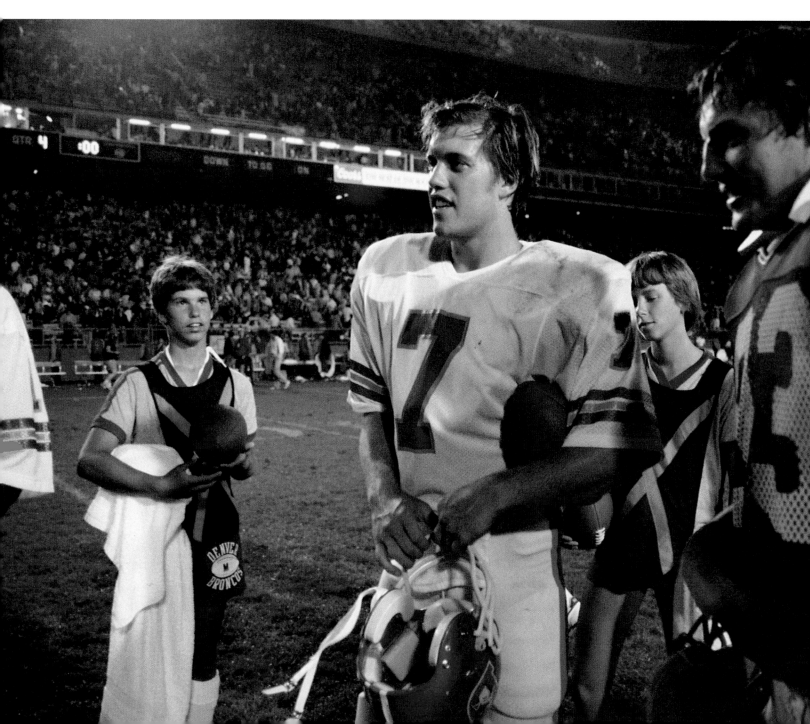

In his Broncos career, John Elway has engineered 41 fourth-quarter game-saving drives and the team has a 40-0-1 record in those games. If that isn't dramatic enough, consider that 21 of those came with less than three minutes remaining, 19 under two minutes and 12 times with less than a minute left. It is so remarkable that NFL Films has issued a videocassette of Elway's Great Saves.

But the most memorable has left an indelible mark in Broncos Folklore; the Drive at Cleveland in the 1986 AFC Championship Game. It was a cold, damp day with a windchill of five degrees. With the clock ticking down and the Broncos behind 20-13, Elway announced in the huddle on his own 2-yard line, "We've got 'em just where we want 'em." Fifteen plays later and with 39 seconds left, Elway hit Mark Jackson for the tying touchdown. In overtime, Elway then directed a 60-yard drive for Rich Karlis to kick the game-winning field goal. Broncos win, 23-20, and head to the Super Bowl.

Janet Reeves, Rocky Mtn. News (2)

There was 5:32 left in the game when Elway began The Drive—a series of 14 plays that took the ball 98 yards for the score. Just as important, it used up all but 37 seconds of regulation time and the Browns were unable to capitalize on the remaining time.

Elway signaled the touchdown with the likelihood of the decision coming in overtime. The Broncos were in control now and the Browns were unable to move the ball in the first series of overtime.

It came down to a 33-yard Rich Karlis kick and it was perfect. Holder Gary Kubiak signaled the score and as the Broncos celebrated, 79,915 partisan Cleveland fans filed quietly from the stadium.

Elway and tackle Dave Studdard happily display the AFC championship trophy on the plane home.

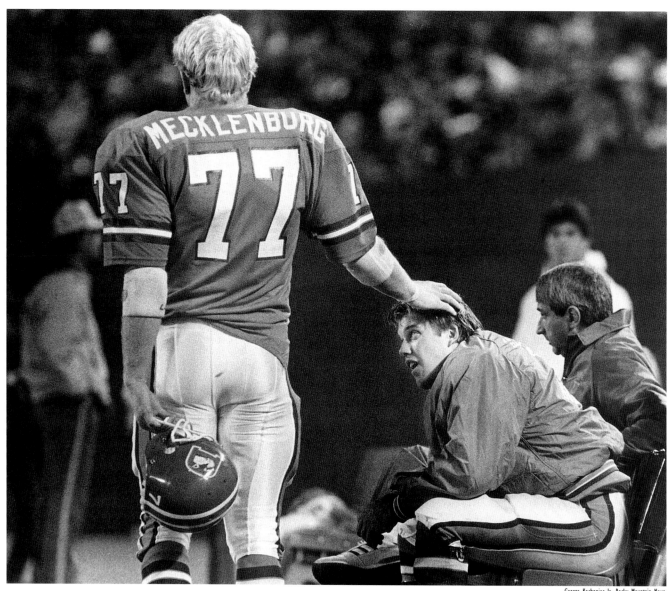

George Kochaniec Jr., Rocky Mountain News

THROUGH 15 YEARS,

NO ONE HAS HAD

THE TOUCH LIKE

JOHN ELWAY

Special players have special regards for each other. Karl Mecklenburg played at an exceptional level for his 11 years with the Broncos and shared moments with John Elway just as Elway saluted Terrell Davis during the 1997 season.

Ryan McKee

OH, BUB, YOU DID IT

By Janet Elway

John and Janet met at Stanford, where she was a swimmer and he was on both the football and baseball teams.

We are normal people living abnormal lives.

Indeed, winning a Super Bowl is not a normal experience. John and I understand this perfectly.

If we believed we deserved any of this, we'd be fooling ourselves in a major way. For whatever reason, God has given me John and given John this great talent. The timing has been right and John has had the right people around him. But he didn't just wave a wand. He has worked very, very hard. In turn, I have worked very, very hard to keep all of the public life and craziness away from us.

John is such a grounded person. We've had so many amazing things happen and John always just laughs and says, "I'd rather be lucky than good." Me, too.

Let's be perfectly honest: With all the money John has made, we do have wonderful things. We have this gorgeous home here in Denver, a home in Palm Desert, a cabin in the mountains, just wonderful stuff. But the far larger point is John works to be the best at whatever he does. The money simply represents a reward for hard work and success.

But it's not the money. What it is is a great life.

Above all, we have always known that if you don't have the love we have and the faith and trust we have in each other, all the *stuff* can be really hollow.

Thinking back on the 1997 season, it's a blur. With football teams, sometimes you get a feeling how a year will really go. I did not have that feeling about last year. I guess after 15 years, I just kind of put the guard up. In the back of my mind I had convinced myself it was too much of a Cinderella story for us to win the Super Bowl.

I hadn't talked myself *totally* out of the idea we could make it to the Super Bowl. But to be brutally candid, I thought it was fantasy what with John being so close to retirement to have him get one more chance and then once he had the chance, to go there and actually win.

I didn't admit this to John. Nor did I admit it to anyone else. Of course, such a horrible thought would never enter John's mind.

John said before and during the season, "If we're gonna do it, this is the time." He felt strongly that having Mike Shanahan, Gary Zimmerman, the talented defense we had, and everyone healthy gave the team an excellent chance. Plus, having Terrell Davis at running back was such a relief. John sensed that everything was in order.

Watching John play and seeing in his eyes how relaxed and how motivated he was started to get me into that mode that he can do anything and so anything can happen. The team just might be able to do it.

The greatest thing about the year, though, is it didn't have to be all John. There was so much team support and John was one of the team. He did his part. The others did, too.

As the year progressed, I was very nervous about the Pittsburgh playoff game. The Steelers quarterback, Kordell Stewart, scared me. I was afraid he'd be the one to find a way to beat us.

However, there also was the fact that our children (Jessie, 12; Jordan, 11; Jack, 8; and Juju, 7) had such blind faith. They were saying, "So when's the Super Bowl? Will we miss school?" This was even before the Wild Card playoff game. They just thought that since we had made it that far, we would go on. Blind faith can be a wonderful thing. I got caught up in the way they think—a little.

At the Super Bowl, it's hard for wives. We not only are handling the family but dealing with all the friends who are there who want to be a part of it—and we want them to be a part of it. But it's a lot of juggling. It helped that the Broncos did a really great job of handling things, too.

Game tickets, plane tickets, hotels. Those are the last things I want John thinking about. You feel responsible for all these people. And they want to know all kinds of things, like, "How do I get to the game? Where can we see John afterward?" I want to take all that I can away from John.

Then you are under the stress and pressure of the game itself.

The way life goes, the 1998 Super Bowl seems too good to be true. It is so amazing that it took place. Going into it, I kept reminding myself that

second place is pretty good. The problem is there is such a huge gap between first and second in sports.

And there we were, playing the Packers. Thinking about John's "better lucky than good" philosophy, I felt like we might have to be really lucky. A lot of people didn't think much of our chances since the previous Super Bowls had not been good for us. But John always feels positive and optimistic. For him, the previous Super Bowls had nothing to do with this Super Bowl. That's why I look to him for wisdom and advice. He's usually about six months ahead of me.

At the game in San Diego, I was sitting in not very good seats, about the 10-yard line, quite high. I had my kids sitting with me and my dad. As it turned out, I couldn't sit anyway. I paced the entire game. The only way I knew what was going on was through the loudspeaker. They did have TVs around so every once in a while I'd look at them for the replays after I'd heard what happened.

I finally sat down for the last five minutes of the game, with my head in my lap. Jessie was holding one hand, Jordan the other. I was shak-

ing. They kept rubbing my back and saying, "Mom, it's going to be okay. We're going to win. You can watch." They told me later I was squeezing their hands so hard that my rings were hurting their little fingers. They were so sweet they didn't want to tell me.

It took down to the last second for me to believe that we won. I was in shock. We were all crying.

I was watching the ceremony afterward from my seat. I suddenly realized that we could go down on the field and that we should go. So I started running down there, collecting members of my family as we ran through the stadium.

First thing John said, "Hey, there you are." I remember saying, "Oh, Bub, you did it. You really did it." We both got teary. There were photographers all around and John put little Jack up on his shoulders. People were crushing us. I was afraid for the kids. It was scary.

And wonderful.

John and I often had talked about what it would be like if he ended his career without a Super Bowl ring. He always said he would know in his heart he would have done everything in his power to win it and he would not have any regret or resentment if he didn't. There is so much involved. He's a big boy. He knows all about these things.

One of the factors that helps John and me is that we met when we were freshmen at Stanford. So we have grown together with all of this. The first time we saw each other, I was at swimming practice and John was on his way to baseball practice. Neither one of us was impressed with the other. Somebody said to me, 'Hey, that's John Elway. I looked at him and shrugged, "That's John Elway?" And when I got out of the pool, John said, "She looks like a little wet rat."

John has most enjoyed sharing his football moments with son Jack, who was eight years old during the Super Bowl season.

Eric Lars Bakke

Eric Lars Bakke

The whole Elway family enjoyed the moment when the team returned from Pittsburgh knowing they were on their way to San Diego.

But we found the beauty in each other.

Another factor that helps our relationship is I am very, very comfortable in a supportive role. I totally believe in that as my position. I feel that is my job and my reality, to be there to love and support him and the kids. I don't feel any need to go off and be somebody. I am comfortable in who I am.

I understand many women do not share my feelings and that's fine. But my Christian values are such that I am relaxed with myself. I believe totally in John and who he is, not only as a football player but as a person with a great mind. I would never get in his way. I only want to be there to complement and help things move along in the best way possible.

It's a big life, being married to John Elway. I'm not sitting home knitting for a lot of reasons, among them that I don't know how to knit.

But we always make sure to nurture our relationship. I don't need the quantity of time from John but we need to make sure the quality is

there. We need to make sure we put our marriage first—and we do. I don't want him totally doting on me and being dedicated to only me and just me. Just nurture the marriage. That's all.

I'm used to him not being around. I have never put a rope on him. I would never try to pull him in or stop him from his successes. I have a feeling John is going to continue to be pulled in lots of directions and continue to be a very successful man. He is not going to be home with me and the kids as much as he'd like. He is off being John Elway and I want him to do that. I would never get in his way. I really believe that.

I know I can sound sappy but this is me. And I'm a really good mom.

Sometimes when he is hanging around the house, he'll try to suggest how to clean the place or discipline the kids. I think, "Wait a minute. This is my territory and I'm the queen of the castle. You're the king but I get the say on my terrain."

I'm pleased that our children seem comfortable with who they are, too. They understand they are John Elway's children but that doesn't define who they are. It's just part of the package.

John guards himself with the public. People don't know the real John. He protects his privacy to the point where he will answer the questions and do what he needs to do, sign autographs, all that. But the John I know is very different. When he walks through the door, he's John my husband, John the dad. I love it that he doesn't give himself to the public. What he does is save himself for me, our family and good friends. I love who he is, not his labels. He doesn't share his heart and soul with anyone except me.

What generally works best is we do a lot of entertaining, almost always impromptu, here at the house. I love to cook. Gatherings usually include our kids, friends, all sorts of people. John truly is the Master of the Barbecue. He cooks hot dogs, hamburgers, marinated steaks, pork tenderloin and he's getting pretty good at ribs. He has had problems with chicken but he's getting better.

What we both like the best is just to sit right here in this house and talk to each other, about the events of the day, about the children, about the wonderful and exciting things in life.

John's heroes in his life are his mom, Jan, and his dad, Jack. From Day One, he wanted to be like them. They have always been there, at every transition. His relationship with them is one of the most special in this life. It's such a gift. They give John foresight and wisdom and they love one another dearly.

When John was deciding whether to retire, Jack and I would sit right here in the kitchen. I respect Jack more than life itself. John would be off reading the paper. Jack and I would debate the decision. John would listen. What it came down to is we felt that John needed to follow what was in his heart. He needed to think about who he is and what's important to him. The main point was Jack and I kept saying, "You don't owe anybody anything. It just needs to be your decision and there's not a bad decision to make here."

What John was doing was testing his heart, trying to see where it lay.

Eventually, John and I were sitting in a restaurant, talking about what to do. And he finally said, "I need to play. I can play. I can do this." That was fine with me. He loves the game, his mind and his body are in great shape and he's not ready to quit.

With his decision, I like the idea that the kids can share their dad's football experience as they get older, especially our little Jack. Watching how much he loves football and now being old enough to understand who his dad is is very nice for him.

In retrospect, it seems like winning the Super Bowl happened so fast. Then we looked around and said, "Since you won, are you done?" With John playing another year, it gives us all a transition year. We will savor everything.

We are not smug because life holds strange twists and turns. What we are, above all, is enormously grateful.

Janet Elway earned her degree in sociology in 1983 from Stanford. She married John on March 3, 1984, in the Menlo Park (Calif.) Presbyterian Church. She spends endless hours chauffeuring the Elway's four children and the inside of her van, to John's dismay, is the mirror image of a landfill.

IN THE FRENZY AFTER THE SUPER BOWL, JOHN, JANET AND DAUGHTER JORDAN SHARED A SPECIAL MOMENT BEFORE AN NBC INTERVIEW.

Ryan McKee

The elapsed time between July in Greeley and January in San Diego seemed like eons. In retrospect, it was a time of assembling many pieces, of maturing as with a fine wine, mixing in a little luck at crucial points and then topping the effort with a frosting of excellence. The result was the Broncos' Super Season.

Not that it was an easy season or that the outcome was at any point sure. In fact, Denver arrived at the Super Bowl as a Wild Card team having to play the Kansas City Chiefs a second time in six weeks in Arrowhead Stadium.

Then it was to Pittsburgh for the second time in four weeks on their home field.

But with adversity came tenacity. And exceptional leadership. And a running back to complement the quarterback's game. And an offensive line. And a defense.

And in the end, a Super Bowl trophy.

THERE WERE TIMES

TO CELEBRATE AND

THE SALUTE BECAME A

Terrell Davis (left), Rod Smith (right) and Derick Dodge (below) all had occasion to throw their hands up in joy.

David Gonzales

SIGNATURE OF THE

SEASON.

David Gonzales

The great October snowstorm tested the ingenuity of players and coaches to get to the Dove Valley headquarters, the airport and ten hours late to Buffalo for their game.

Quiet intensity are words often used describing Mike Shanahan's demeanor. He is comfortable with owner Pat Bowlen's presence in the locker room and gathers players in moments of contemplation and prayer before and after games.

SHANAHAN'S

APPROACH IS

ONE IN WHICH HE IS

NEITHER FRIEND OF

NOR UNDULY FEARED

BY PLAYERS.

Eric Lars Bakke (3)

From sixth-round draft choice to MVP of the Super Bowl, the Terrell Davis story is one that is straight storybook. Yet by the end of the Super Season, Davis had become the dependable producer of massive yardage, numbers to be expected each week. The records seemed to fall by the week and 100-yard games were routine.

It was midseason when Davis passed the 5,000-yard career mark but it was in the Super Bowl that he rushed for a record three touchdowns and 157 yards, all this while leaving the game for 15 minutes with a migraine headache that left him without sight momentarily.

Luckily, eyesight returned and so did Davis.

For Davis, it was a San Diego homecoming for a football career begun at that city's Lincoln High. From there, on to Long Beach State and, eventually, the University of Georgia before becoming the 196th pick in the draft.

If only the rest of the NFL knew then what they know now.

THE FLYING DAVIS,

RECORDS FALLING

AS YARDAGE WAS

CLIMBING

CONGRATULATIONS TO

#30 Terrell Davis

HE HAS JUST REACHED

5000

TOTAL YARDS FASTER THAN ANY BRONCO EVER. HE IS ONLY THE 8TH PLAYER EVER TO DO THIS IN HIS FIRST THREE SEASONS.

Ryan McKee

The Mile High scoreboard announced a midseason record.

Trying to bring down Davis was a difficult task for the NFL's best defenders in his third season, here against Oakland and Jacksonville.

There wasn't that much time on the bench for Davis, who carried the ball 369 times during the 1997 season.

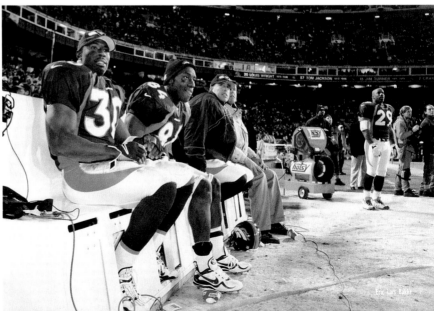

Eric Lars Bakke

Rich Clarkson

The defensive line presented a unified front, both on and off the field.

Bill Romanowski was a lightning rod for controversy while anchoring the Broncos linebacking corps.

Long-time adversary Neil Smith's arrival in Denver was bad news for his former teammates in Kansas City. Here, he celebrated the playoff victory on his former home field.

Cornerback Ray Crockett consistently shut down the league's top receivers.

Eric Lars Bakke

THE SUPER SEASON

OFFENSE INCLUDED

A CORPS OF

RUNNING BACKS

Behind Terrell Davis came more running backs, who looked like anything but back-ups. Derek Loville (left) and Vaughn Hebron (below) both had their moments including the Jacksonville playoff game where both scored and contributed to Denver's 310 rushing yards, best in franchise history.

David Gonzales

One of the contributing factors to Terrell Davis' rushing success in 1997 was the fact that opposing defenses had to respect the Broncos' passing game. Not simply the arm of John Elway, but the group of sure-handed men on the receiving end of Elway's bullets.

For sheer beauty and grace, wide receiver Rod Smith led the way. His one-handed grab at Kansas City is just one of a number of Smith receptions that Broncos fans won't soon forget.

If you like your catches with a dash of grit, then wide receiver Ed McCaffrey is your kind of player. Time and time again, McCaffrey's willingness to sacrifice his body resulted in key plays.

And, of course, there's unparalleled tight end Shannon Sharpe. The defining player at his position in the '90s, Sharpe earned a sixth Pro Bowl selection in 1997 and the continued grudging admiration of defensive coordinators around the league who have yet to figure out how to cover him.

POSITION, AGILITY,

CONCENTRATION,

ALL MUST COMBINE

PERFECTLY WITH

THE DELIVERY

Once Ed McCaffrey has the ball, he seems to seek out contact.

David Gonzales

Rod Smith gathers the ball against the Patriots – and an out-of-position defender.

Shannon Sharpe hauled in more passes than any other Broncos receiver.

Ryan McKee

David Gonzales

*Elway's receiving corps hauled
in 27 touchdown passes on the year—
a franchise record.*

*Ed McCaffrey's ability to pick up extra yards
was evident in every contest (above right).*

*Rod Smith (above far right) led the squad
with 12 touchdown grabs.*

*Third receiver Willie Green (right) stepped
up in the regular season showdown at Kansas City,
setting up the Broncos' late go-ahead field goal with
a pair of catches.*

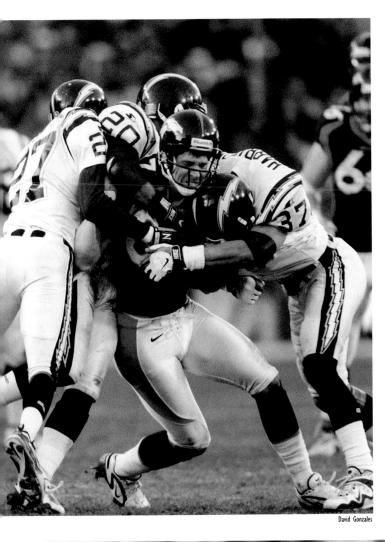

David Gonzales

Eric Lars Bakke

David Gonzales

The saying is that defense wins championships, and the 1997 Broncos did nothing to disprove that adage. True, the three-headed offensive juggernaut of Elway, Davis and Sharpe grabbed much of the spotlight. But at the end of many games it was the defense on the field preserving the victory—as they did at Kansas City in the playoffs and against Green Bay in Super Bowl XXXII.

A strong 1996 squad was made even stronger in the offseason through the free-agent acquisitions of Darrien Gordon, former Bronco Keith Traylor, and longtime Denver nemesis Neil Smith. The emergence of young stars like John Mobley and Maa Tanuvasa complemented the steady play of veterans like Steve Atwater and Tyrone Braxton. And true professionals such as Bill Romanowski and Ray Crockett could always be counted on to "leave it all on the field."

The Broncos were best in the AFC in yards allowed and tied a franchise record for touchdown returns with 10 in 1997. But they will perhaps be best remembered for one play—Mobley's deflection of Brett Favre's fourth-down pass that sealed the team's first-ever world championship.

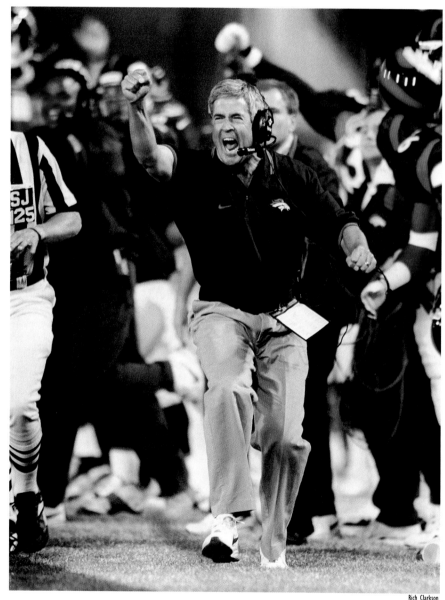

Rich Clarkson

Defensive coordinator Greg Robinson's troops found themselves under attack most of the season, but still led the conference in total defense.

A smothering defense was led here by Keith Traylor (94) and Allen Aldridge (57).

THE OFFENSE MAY
HAVE GOTTEN THE
HEADLINES, BUT IT WAS
THE DEFENSE THAT
STEPPED UP TO SEAL
MANY DENVER WINS.

Free-agent acquisition Darrien Gordon (right) made his mark with four interceptions and four returns for touchdowns.

Cornerback Ray Crockett's 21 passes defensed was nearly twice as many as anyone else on the team.

1997 was second-year linebacker John Mobley's breakthrough season, as he led the Broncos with 162 tackles.

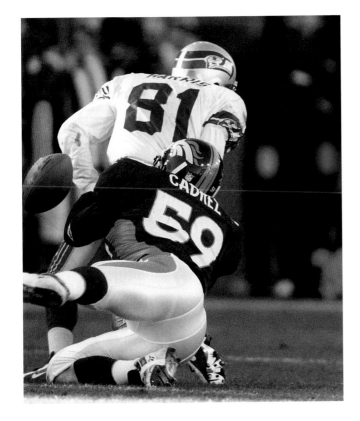

Linebacker Glenn Cadrez (upper left) helped man an equally punishing special teams unit.

A return to the Pro Bowl was in store for defensive end Neil Smith (above) after racking up 8.5 sacks on the season.

With safeties Tyrone Braxton (left) and Steve Atwater patrolling the secondary, opposing receivers often found themselves separated from the football.

Eric Lars BAkke

*The Patriots thought they could go
head-to-head with the Broncos defense in
the preseason . . .*

*. . . but they found nowhere to run in the
regular-season rematch.*

David Gonzales

A MONDAY NIGHT MAULING AT
MILE HIGH SENT THE
MESSAGE THAT THE
BALANCE OF POWER IN THE
AFC HAD TIPPED TO THE WEST.

David Gonzales

Ryan McKee

Denver's 1996 season ended on the sourest of notes as the upstart Jacksonville Jaguars came to their first ever playoff game and upset the heavily favored Broncos 30-27. A pall fell over Denver the rest of the winter.

History began to repeat itself in 1997 with the first playoff opponent again being Jacksonville. No one in Denver could forget the previous year.

The Broncos wasted no time jumping to touchdowns on each of their first three possessions. Terrell Davis ran for 184 yards before an injury, so backup running back Derek Loville came in for another 103 of Denver's season record 310 rushing yards. A Jacksonville comeback faltered and Denver went on to a decisive 42-17 win.

What goes around comes around.

Backup running back Derek Loville celebrated with reason; substituting for the injured Terrell Davis, he scored two touchdowns.

THE SECRET TO DENVER'S

1997 SUCCESS IS SIMPLE.

BIG PLAYERS MADE

BIG PLAYS IN BIG GAMES.

Ryan McKee

John Elway hit Rod Smith for a 43-yard touchdown over the middle. Later, son Jack celebrated the victory with his dad in the locker room.

Tradition joins youth each season as the Broncos faithful pour into Mile High Stadium for the celebration of NFL football. Broncos mascot Thunder gallops down the field after touchdowns. This edition of the mascot, officially registered as "JB Kobast," is a 14-year old Arabian stallion from Ft. Lupton ridden by Angela Moore. But for longevity, the "Barrel Man," Tim McKernan, must hold some kind of team record. When he first began leading cheers in the stands, there was not a white hair on his head. But then, some Broncos finishes will lead to premature graying.

Fans filled Mile High for more than just the games—the team's triumphant return from San Diego drew thousands of Broncos faithful.

David Gonzales

A leg injury kept team mascot Thunder off the field for the regular season, but he was back in time to celebrate the playoff win over Jacksonville.

Eric Lars Bakke

The hair may have a little more gray, but Barrel Man is still a familiar sight.

ANK TRIPUCKA 1960-1963   OWNER GERALD H. PHIPPS 1961-1981   87 RICH JACKSC

Ryan McKee

David Gonzales

A second straight undefeated regular season at home gave the crowd plenty to cheer about . . .

David Gonzales

. . . as the Broncos proved that they truly were a mile above the rest in more ways than one.

HE CAN DO IT ALL

Eric Lars Bakke

Shanahan's tenure in San Francisco showed him how important a healthy relationship between the head coach and starting quarterback can be.

By Bill Walsh

Mike Shanahan is the rarest of coaches in the National Football League: He can do it all.

The basic reason he led the Broncos to their Super Bowl win was his complete knowledge of the technical aspects of the game, which is probably the single most important category when it comes to players appreciating, recognizing and respecting the coach. This is what the players respond to the most. I can't stress this enough. It's not someone who can give a slick presentation who wins in the NFL. It's a person who knows his business and can do his job well.

Players spot a phony in a heartbeat. They know Mike Shanahan is no phony.

Mike is one of just a handful of coaches who have this high level of credibility and he brings it to everything he does. Consequently, the players begin to believe in him almost immediately. His credibility is related to his experiences, to his own philosophies and to his knowledge of technical football. Then on top of all this, Mike has a system of football that is complete and he can teach every nuance and every technique and every skill involved. So he brings total and complete expertise in the field of coaching and managing a football team.

The list goes on and on. Success came to Denver because Mike brought strict organization to the football operation. He's also an excellent judge of talent and he's a great strategist. The players see all of this, including his game management, and they immediately have a belief in what he can bring to them and the service he can perform for them during the game.

These are *some* of the things all of us would like to think we can bring to a team; but in Mike's case, he does. He can fully mobilize an organization and an operation. And because of his intensity and his ability to communicate, people will follow him. He's a natural leader. I don't use the word inspiration often because sometimes that's pretty short-lived. But, yes, Mike can be extremely inspiring.

Mike manages things so well that everyone—well, okay, almost everyone—plays at his full potential.

He created the proper and necessary atmosphere in Denver because he brings enthusiasm to the task. But it's no-nonsense enthusiasm. In other words, he thrives on his role of head coach. Football to him is not just a lot of people having fun, although Mike's definitely not against fun. In fact, he's refreshing and enthusiastic and he can smile and he can thoroughly enjoy what he's doing and the people around him. It's just that his is a very serious approach to things with a complete commitment to detail and to improving the skills of each player every day. What happens is the players can see and envision themselves performing better because of him.

They also see that because Mike is able to do his job so well as a strategist and as a teacher, the environment improves dramatically. Now it was good before, no question about that. Denver has had some solid coaches. But everyone was inspired by what Mike could bring to the team. They found themselves fully committed to what he was requiring of them.

He's a truly dedicated professional. But he's not a tedious person nor a person who is tediously redundant.

Our connection started when he coached the Raiders. I was an NBC broadcaster and Mike had been sort of isolated in that role. He was having great difficulties with that job. Since I had just left the 49ers and had a good track record, Mike and I identified with each other very quickly. I think I served as a good resource for him during those very difficult and troubling times with the Raiders.

There's no question he was worried he would be "damaged goods" after the Raider experience. Everyone feels that way. Mike was very sober to the possibility he might never have another opportunity. The problem is that when you appear to have failed at one head coaching job it may be a while, if ever, that you have an opportunity again. Conceivably, he might find himself back at the college level before returning to the NFL. There isn't any question you feel a real loss of esteem when these kinds of things occur. But very often, when people get that second opportunity, they are much better prepared.

At that time, I knew he had so much to offer. It's just the circumstances weren't right at the Raiders.

So what he needed to do was find his way from that situation to a very good one. Serving at Denver and then with the 49ers as an assistant coach added to his knowledge of the game and gave him experiences that would really be a profit to him when he became—hopefully—a head coach again.

When Mike subsequently became offensive coordinator at San Francisco, we worked together on him developing his understanding of the offense so he'd have a complete inventory of knowledge. Then we worked on how to handle the personnel. And we'd periodically visit about his career progress. Later, I was a factor in Mike taking on the Denver job, which was one of a number of opportunities he had. Seattle wanted him. San Francisco wanted

him to stay and eventually be the head coach. San Diego was interested. He was the hottest property in the National Football League at the time he joined the Broncos.

We talked along the way about how to get along with owners. We had conversations in this regard relating to the Raiders, the 49ers and the Broncos. In considering head coaching opportunities and possibilities, we discussed the ownerships and how attractive it would be to work for different owners.

Being at the 49ers catapulted him to an elite position because they had been so successful and others have done so well as head coaches after being with the 49ers. And Mike personally is so capable and so attractive that he was ideally situated. So when the 49ers

won the Super Bowl in 1994, that set him in perfect position.

Fortunately, Denver was in the perfect position to rehire Mike. It also was fortunate that the Broncos had such a prominent, knowledgeable and professional owner as Pat Bowlen.

It pleases me enormously that we have become professional colleagues— and friends.

When Mike took the Denver job, he flew in to see me. We spent considerable time talking about how he should establish himself as the head coach of the Broncos. The best part was that when he took over, everything was in place including the facilities and an outstanding quarterback in John Elway. The Broncos needed Mike and Mike needed the Broncos. It was a perfect matchup.

Shanahan can shed his quiet demeanor to fire up the team when necessary while still treating players with respect.

Perhaps the main thing is Mike had something to offer John Elway. Of course, John had an awful lot to offer football, the Broncos and Mike. But Mike had something that connected with John Elway, and that was a tutelage that could enhance his performances, to the point where John became one of just a handful of truly great players in football. John appreciated what Mike could provide. There are very few men in football coaching who John Elway would truly respect because John is so far along as a great player that he can easily identify whether someone can really help him with his game.

It takes an absolute expert to help a truly great player. That's what Mike could provide John Elway.

But Mike, of course, has to deal with all the players and he's able to do this because his personality is flexible, positive and supportive. With Mike there isn't any hidden agenda. He's honest and forthright with his athletes. He can be trusted and the players sense that.

A huge advantage that Denver had in its Super Bowl year was the far-reaching abilities of Mike. The more able the coach, the more complete and thorough the strategy. The Broncos had been on the edge of finding themselves all year, maturing as a team. Yet, it didn't look good at times in 1997, especially when the Broncos had to go on the road in the playoffs. Ultimately, some of it, I suppose, is good fortune. But what they did was time it just right. They got healthy at the end and found themselves physically. They had a tough road to San Diego and that seasoned them and toughened them. Because of this road traveled, they went into the Super Bowl positive about themselves and why they were there.

They were at their very best at the Super Bowl.

Elway went into the game without a heck of a lot of pressure. He didn't have to carry the mantle of favorite or someone the people assumed would win, like Brett Favre did. John played loose and easy. What he did was perform. As long as an organization is well structured, well coached—and you have Elway—you have a chance.

John was at his best in the toughest games at the end of the year.

So what's ahead for Denver? Who knows. But there aren't any dynasties in football any longer. The competition will be even keener this year than last, especially in the AFC. I believe the AFC will become the dominant conference and will demonstrate it this year. They have a number of very strong teams. In the AFC West, there are a group of solid, competitive football teams. The Raiders will be much improved, Seattle will be much better, Kansas City will be solid again, San Diego will be improved.

And certainly the Broncos can win again, but they may have to win the same way again. It might very well be that Denver struggles as the season progresses. But other teams will struggle, too, because parity is everywhere. Maybe the Broncos will have an 11-5 or 10-6 record, possibly winning their division and possibly not, then being at their best at the close of the season. And, because of their Super Bowl success, they should have the poise and presence to play even better in the playoff games.

When it comes to repeating as champions, we've seen the Chicago Bulls. So, we have a precedent. I'm sure that Mike will remind his players over and over about how the Bulls have done so well.

I'd say Mike's biggest problem is that it's really tough to get down to business again even though you know you should. That you *must.* The euphoria extends well into the next season. To refocus is very, very difficult because no matter what kind of attention you give it, you still are overcome by such a heady experience. Everybody is— coaches, ownership, players. Refocusing may take some time. That's why it could appear that the Broncos aren't headed anywhere in the midpoint in

Eric Lars Bakke

In the locker room, Shanahan can inspire with a quiet intensity.

the season, then will find themselves and be ready to make another run.

Often it takes some new talent to revitalize a winning team and improve it. Then it takes complete focus on the part of everyone. Elway's leadership will be very important. Mike must make sure he continues to pay strict attention to detail and his expectations for his team have to be even higher. He has to demonstrate how he is personally totally committed and demanding of the players. You can tighten up on the players when you're winning. It's harder when you're losing.

At this point, I'm dead certain the players believe in Mike.

I wish Elway had indicated he would play two more years, even if he meant one, so that the pressure wouldn't be on him in every town he plays this season. Everywhere he goes, it will be the last time to see Elway. He'll feel that.

Sometimes being a coach is overwhelming. Often you are just operating on nerves. You are totally consumed. The only way you can effectively deal with it, which Mike is quite able to do, is compartmentalize each demand that is made on you and each issue that is out there. You do this so you don't let some frustrating things affect everything else.

However, it's not all Mike. His other coaches have to be totally focused. They are the ones who do the vast majority of the individual coaching. That's going to be a real challenge for Mike. He has to make sure they are not distracted by their recent success. You have to be careful it doesn't become an atmosphere of euphoric fellowship but one of hard work.

We visited extensively during the offseason about what considerations there are when you return from a Super Bowl championship. He wanted some ideas about indicators that you are not focused. He wanted some thoughts on what approach should be taken in demands he makes on the players. A big advantage is Mike is seasoned now.

The core of my message to Mike was that you can't make too much of winning the Super Bowl. That's hard, of course, and to a certain degree impossible. But what you have to do is make sure you get back to work.

When it comes strictly to football, Mike's most pleased when there's a perfectly executed play, hopefully one he has designed and installed. He is most frustrated, win or lose, when his team doesn't execute well, because he's a detail man. He thrives on the technical aspects. There can be games that the Broncos win and he is relieved but he is not at all happy and is somewhat embarrassed by the performance and execution.

There are plenty of other coaches who just don't have the depth and appreciation of the game. Somehow if they win, they are elated, but they don't even know why they won. In Mike's case, winning with precision execution is what gives him the most gratification.

As the years pass, he will become one of the two or three preeminent coaches in football. As time tests him, and he continues to establish a pattern of success, I believe he'll be a Hall of Fame football coach. But Mike would be the first one to point out that's way down the field and life teaches that there are plenty of chances for slips between the cup and the lip.

When Bill Walsh became head coach of the San Francisco 49ers in 1979, they were coming off a 2-14 year. Just three years later, they were 16-3 and won the Super Bowl. During Walsh's 10-year reign, he led San Francisco to three Super Bowl titles. He's now a member of the Pro Football Hall of Fame.

David Gonzales

Gary Kubiak is typical of Shanahan's key assistants who bring experience and respect to their specialties, complementing the head coach's leadership. Kubiak, now offensive coordinator, was Elway's backup quarterback for eight years.

David Gonzales

Combine the Broncos' 35th appearance on *Monday Night Football* with the city's most-hated opponent—the Oakland Raiders—and the intensity level is on high. It seems that when ABC brings its cameras to Mile High Stadium, there is always a special flavor.

This year, there was no snowstorm nor last-minute heroics. There was just the Raiders. And nothing suited the Broncos more than to rub a little salt in Al Davis' wounds with a decisive 31-3 victory. The rivalry between the two teams has been intense from the first days of the old AFL. Then all Broncos fans knew well the story of Mike Shanahan's experience as Raiders head coach and that only added to the feelings. Strange that a blowout victory ranks as one of the season highlights. But then, sending the Raiders and Davis packing is always a Denver highlight.

Return man Darrien Gordon (right) had a busy night, as the Denver defense forced Oakland to punt the ball away eight times.

RAIDERS

Ryan McKee

David Gonzales

Broncos fans left no doubt about their position . . .

. . . on coach Shanahan's dispute with his former boss—Al Davis.

Ryan McKee

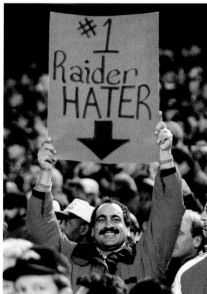

Eric Lars BAkke

A 38-year rivalry is still going strong.

Terrell Davis tied a franchise record with three rushing touchdowns.

Ryan McKee

THE BRONCOS PILED UP

280 YARDS THROUGH THE

AIR, LED BY SHANNON

SHARPE'S 10 CATCHES

FOR 142 YARDS.

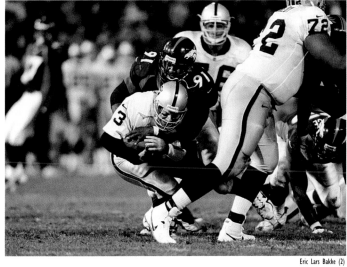

Defensive end Alfred Williams (left) tallied one of Denver's four sacks on the night.

Eric Lars Bakke (2)

Dwayne Carswell (below) and the Broncos coverage teams kept return threat Desmond Howard in check.

NOTHING BRINGS OUT

THE "FANATIC" IN

BRONCOS FANS LIKE A

MONDAY NIGHT

MATCHUP AGAINST THE

SILVER AND BLACK.

Eric Lars Bakke

The action in the parking lot and the stands was nearly as intense as on the field.

Eric Lars Bakke

Ryan Mckee

Even National League MVP Larry Walker joined the festivities.

In the regular season of 1997, the traditional rivalry with the Kansas City Chiefs was played out to a draw, much to the displeasure of Broncos fans. As the season began, the Broncos controlled the game in Denver and crafted a decisive 19-3 win with a solid defensive display. But when the rematch was played in November, Denver suffered a heartbreaking 24-22 defeat at the hands—or more appropriately, the feet of the Chiefs when Pete Stoyanovich connected on a 54-yard field goal as time ran out. Elway had just led another last-minute drive to put Denver ahead 22-21 with only a minute remaining. But that was enough for the Chiefs to put their kicker in position to win the game. It was a bitter loss, but it was to be avenged.

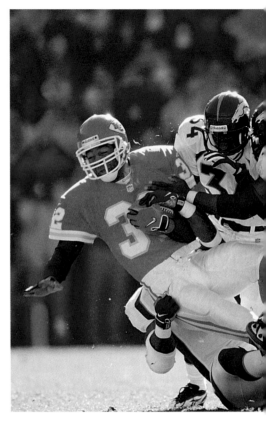

The Denver defense held Kansas City running back Marcus Allen (right) to under 3 yards per carry.

Life wasn't any easier for John Elway, who was sacked six times.

Eric Lars Bakke

The Broncos moved the ball well, but had trouble getting in the end zone.

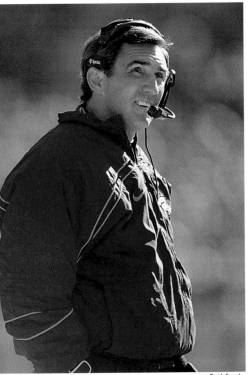

David Gonzales

Coach Shanahan (above) watched apprehensively as Pete Stoyanovich's 54-yard field goal barely sailed over the crossbar.

A jubilant Stoyanovich was carried triumphantly off the field after his game-winning kick.

Eric Lars Bakke

David Gonzales

David Gonzal

The third Kansas City game was the most important, for it held a place in The AFC Championship Game for the victor. The Chiefs had the home-field advantage and were favorites because of it. It was to be the first road playoff win for the Broncos in 11 years, but not an easy one. Two Terrell Davis touchdowns and a defensive effort that tied a club playoff record for fewest points resulted in the Broncos victory. Chiefs quarterback Elvis Grbac was pressured all day long as the Kansas City game plan was interrupted again and again. But it wasn't until the final play of the game that the outcome was sure. The Chiefs were in scoring position. That was when the potential game-winning pass was knocked down by Darrien Gordon, giving the Broncos the 14-10 win. On to Pittsburgh.

FORMER CHIEF NEIL SMITH ENJOYED HIS BEST PERFORMANCE AGAINST HIS OLD TEAM- MATES WITH TWO SACKS AND A FORCED FUMBLE.

Safety Steve Atwater (left) and a stingy Broncos defense helped Denver post its first road playoff win in 11 years.

Terrell Davis (below) led the way with 101 yards rushing and both Denver touchdowns.

David Gonzales

Eric Lars Bakke

Tight end Shannon Sharpe left the stunned Arrowhead crowd with a farewell gesture after the game.

David Gonzales

A KEY THIRD-DOWN

CATCH BY ROD SMITH

(RIGHT) LED TO THE

FIRST SCORE OF

THE GAME.

David Gonzales

Kansas City's desperation fourth-down pass to the end zone was thwarted by the outstretched fingertips of Darrien Gordon (below).

Cornerback Darrius Johnson (left) and the Denver defense never did rest, tying a franchise postseason record by limiting Kansas City to just 10 points.

David Gonzales

Eric Lars Bakke

David Gonzales

The AFC Championship Game was all that stood in the way of the Broncos' march to the Super Bowl. But it was the Pittsburgh Steelers that stood there, with one-time Coloradan Kordell Stewart and running back Jerome Bettis looming large as offensive threats.

Denver took an early lead on Terrell Davis' 8-yard touchdown run in the first quarter, but Pittsburgh answered immediately with a touchdown drive of its own, culminated by Kordell Stewart's 33-yard run.

The Steelers took a 14-7 lead in the second quarter when Jerome Bettis plowed into the end zone from 1 yard out. Denver trimmed the lead to 14-10 on Jason Elam's 43-yard field goal, then scored 14 points in the last two minutes of the half on two John Elway touchdown passes—one each to Howard Griffith and Ed McCaffrey—to hold a 24-14 lead at the half.

The second half was dominated by the two defenses, as the score remained unchanged until Stewart hooked up with receiver Charles Johnson on a 14-yard scoring pass to bring Pittsburgh within three points with 2:46 remaining. But the Steelers would never see the ball again, as the Broncos offense picked up three first downs to run out the clock and seal the victory.

Denver's defense came up big in the playoffs again, registering three sacks and forcing four turnovers. Davis ran for 139 yards on 26 carries—the only back to gain 100 yards on the ground against the Pittsburgh defense all season. Elway threw for 210 yards and two touchdowns in winning the fourth AFC Championship of his career.

David Gonzales

Terrell Davis became the Broncos' all-time postseason rushing leader with his 139-yard effort.

David Gonzales

MALIGNED AFTER DENVER'S DECEMBER LOSS IN

PITTSBURGH, ROD SMITH AND THE REST OF THE

BRONCOS RECEIVING CORPS CAME BACK WITH ONE

OF THEIR BEST PERFORMANCES OF THE YEAR.

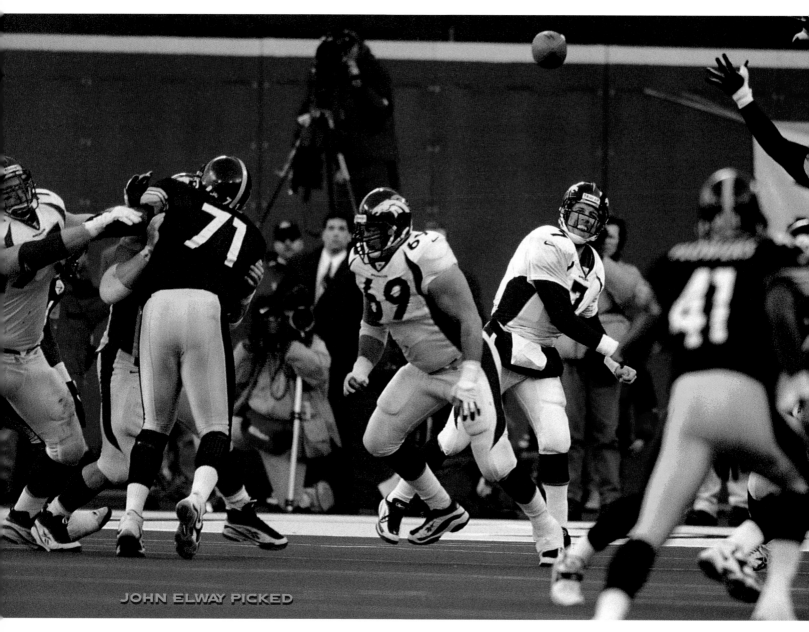

JOHN ELWAY PICKED

APART PITTSBURGH'S

TYPICALLY TOUGH

DEFENSE FOR 210

YARDS AND TWO

TOUCHDOWNS.

Fullback Howard Griffith's second-quarter touchdown put the Broncos ahead for good.

Denver's defense made the lead hold up with big play after big play.

Tight end Shannon Sharpe's third-down reception helped the Broncos run out the clock and preserved the victory.

OWNER PAT BOWLEN

David Gonzales

WAS ALL SMILES AFTER

HIS DEFENSE FORCED

FOUR TURNOVERS EN

ROUTE TO DENVER'S

FIFTH AFC

CHAMPIONSHIP VICTORY.

Eric Lars Bakke

Eric Lars Bakke

THE SMITHS—

NEIL (LEFT) AND ROD

(BELOW)—EXEMPLIFIED

THE TEAM'S FESTIVE

MOOD ON THE FLIGHT

BACK TO DENVER.

David Gonzales

John Elway assured the fans greeting the team at the airport that big things were coming in San Diego.

Eric Lars Bakke

FINALLY, A SUPER BOWL

By Jim Murray, *Los Angeles Times*

David Gonzales

Whew! Finally, a Super Bowl that was Super! As this is written, Roman candles are going off in the air, music is blasting, metallic confetti is blowing through the air.

Disney would love the outcome. The most popular victory since *Bambi.*

America's Sweetheart finally wins one. No dummy, *not* Bill Clinton. John Elway!

The Green Bay Packers were the bad guys in this melodrama. The guys in the black hats.

They went out with their guns drawn and their boots on. They had the ball on the Denver 31 marching to the tying score when a fourth-down pass tipped off the end of a receiver's fingers.

But if you had an ounce of compassion, you were supposed to be for Elway. It was supposed to be another four-handkerchief picture. A tear-jerker for poor John. Where he dies in the fadeout. You had to root for him the same way you rooted for John Wayne or Gary Cooper. The American flag. Apple pie. Motherhood.

So we got the happy ending. This was a horse opera, not grand opera.

But Elway had a sidekick in the best tradition of Hollywood cliff-hangers. This was a guy whose initials translated out, fittingly enough, to "T.D."

Terrell Davis is his name. The Lone Ranger had Tonto. And John Elway had T.D.

Elway passed the ball only 22 times in Super Bowl XXXII. Normally, that's barely a good half for him. But he schlepped the ball out to Davis often enough to make the difference. In the smart game plan, Davis took it in for a record three touchdowns.

"We shocked the world!" crowed Denver's Shannon Sharpe.

In a way, they did. The gamblers took a look and gave you 11 1/2 points if you wanted Denver, heartless wretches that they are.

I'll be honest with you. I expected to be starting this column by writing something like "The Green Bay Packers and the NFC won the Super Bowl on Sunday. And a pie is round, and the sky is blue and the pope is Catholic."

But it ran the wrong way. It turned out man bites dog. No cliché.

It was vintage Elway. In the first quarter, trailing 7-0, he had the ball on the Green Bay 12-yard line. He faded to pass, watched Green Bay peel back frantically to stop it. So, he helped himself to a vital 10 yards and Davis scored two plays later. Another time he started on his 8-yard line and marched the Broncos 92 yards for the score that gave them a 24-17 lead.

The game really was a classic boxer-vs.-puncher. Green Bay was bigger. But Denver was faster. Quicker. If anything, more resourceful.

But if Elway and Davis got carried off on shoulders and bask in a Denver ticker-tape parade, two of the Denver cast of characters found sweet vindication too.

All his career, wide receiver Ed McCaffrey has had an identity crisis. He has had trouble convincing people he's fast enough for the position. Then, of course, he went to Stanford. That's not Miami or Notre Dame. In other words, suspect too.

McCaffrey was on the New York Giants and caught 49 passes one year, with five touchdowns. But the Giants dubbed him a "possession receiver." Translation: sure-handed but slow. He went to San Francisco where they threw to him enough for only 11 catches.

Denver got him because its coach had seen him when both were at San Francisco. Says Coach Mike Shanahan: "We thought here's a 6-5 receiver and as we saw him, he consistently won one-on-ones and could beat bump coverage. So we jumped to get him."

In the middle of the third quarter, with the score 17-17 and Denver gasping, Elway threw two passes to McCaffrey, one for 36 yards and one for 9. They were key in the drive that gave Denver its 24-17 lead.

But if McCaffrey was vindicated, so was the coach who got him, Shanahan.

Mike Shanahan is a strange character in this violent game. He himself was a college player who lost a kidney in a pileup. So he became a coach.

Shanahan is a character who looks more or less like a guy gazing at his own corpse. His eyes look as if they had a line shining behind them. He rarely smiles. He's always going to look 15 years younger than he is (45).

He came to Denver with the reputation of being one of those cerebral types, a coach who draws up plays on the blackboard and is a whiz with the Xs and O's. But he is supposed to stay in his ivory tower and not come out and try to be a field leader. They thought that about Bill Walsh, once, too.

The Raider's Al Davis enticed him away from his drawing board at Denver and made him head coach at L.A. but barely gave him time to learn the names of his secondary before jerking the rug out from under him.

Shanahan came back to Denver as an assistant licking his wounds and embarrassed. But Elway, for one, loved him. Eventually, so did the owner. He made him head coach. If there's one thing that was needed on the Broncos, it was a guy who has John Elway's complete confidence.

Super Bowl XXXII showed that Mike Shanahan is no mad scientist (even if he sometimes looks like one). It showed Ed McCaffrey can get open with the best of them. It showed John Elway can win any game if he has the sidekicks to do it.

It showed that Denver can win at sea level. It showed speed and smarts can neutralize superior strength.

And it showed that a Super Bowl can be a very exciting game. This was a fight between two top heavyweights that had the crowd on its feet. And that it can be won by the guys in white hats, the Public's Choices.

Boffo Box Office.

DENVER FINALLY HAD A

FIRM GRASP ON THE

THING THEY HAD BEEN

REACHING FOR FOR 38

YEARS—A WORLD

CHAMPIONSHIP

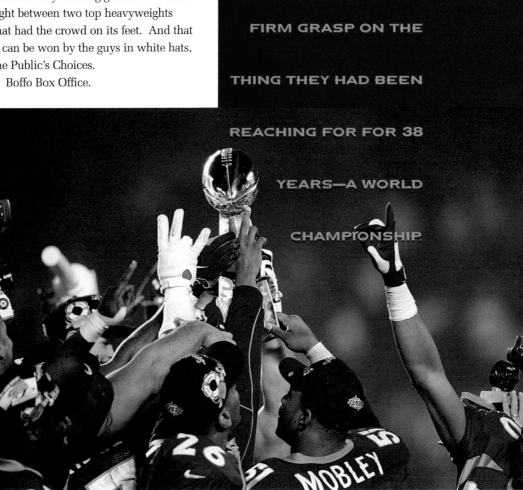

Ryan McKee

GOOD YEAR
#1 in TIRES

Russell Stover

SANYO

Budweiser

FIVE BLIMPS CRUISED

THE SAN DIEGO SKIES

AS SUPER BOWL XXXII

BEGAN

PAGEANTRY, PASSION AND PIGSKINS

The spectacle of Super Bowls has grown since the first in the Los Angeles Coliseum back in 1967. By 1998 in San Diego, the other weeklong events threatened to overwhelm the game itself. But by Sunday afternoon, with the pregame parties, the NFL Experience and press conferences all past, pageantry was called in to pave the way for football. No less than five blimps cruised the sky over Qualcomm Stadium where hundreds of chartered buses and thousands of parked cars peppered the surrounding area. Nearly 70,000 fans heard everything from the Beach Boys to Boyz II Men as hundreds of dancers pranced about. The Blue Angels and a B-2 bomber flew overhead and the national anthem signaled the time for football. It was game time.

David Gonzales

Blimps carrying advertising messages above Super Bowl XXXII's Qualcomm Stadium demonstrate just how much of a spectacle the game has become.

The Broncos Cheerleaders did their part to help will the team to victory.

Chad Slattery

David Gonzales

A PAIR OF ED

MCCAFFREY CATCHES

ACCOUNTED FOR

NEARLY HALF OF

DENVER'S 92 YARDS IN

THEIR THIRD-QUARTER

SCORING DRIVE.

Kick returner Vaughn Hebron (above) gave the Broncos good starting field position throughout the game.

John Elway (left) was completely focused on bringing Denver its first Super Bowl title.

Eric Lars Bakke

FULLBACK HOWARD

GRIFFITH SET UP

DENVER'S WINNING

TOUCHDOWN WITH

HIS 23-YARD CATCH

AND RUN.

David Gonzales

Eric Lars Bakke

Cornerback Tim McKyer (above) nearly put the game away with his third-quarter fumble recovery.

Terrell Davis (left) found the man who had been opening huge holes for him to run through all night and all season after scoring the winning touchdown— Howard Griffith.

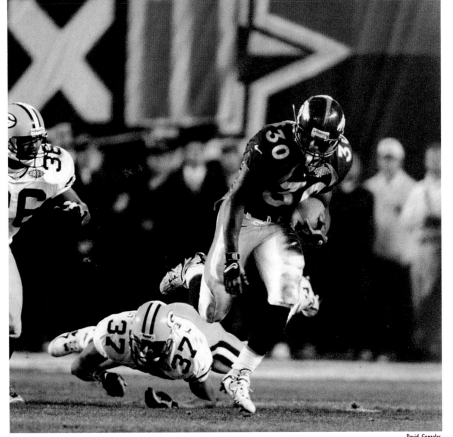

David Gonzales

TERRELL DAVIS LEFT

GREEN BAY DEFEND-

ERS CLUTCHING AT AIR

THE ENTIRE GAME.

David Gonzales

In the second quarter, the Broncos trainers guided Davis from the field after he was hit in the head and blacked out. On the bench, his eyesight was gone for a short time—an offshoot of the migraine headaches he sometimes has. It was 15 minutes before he was able to reenter the game.

What does it take to be Super Bowl MVP?
Try 157 rushing yards and three touchdowns.

Eric Lars Bakke

everyday

4   T   TO
7   3
14   3
33   2 QTR

76

GE SANYO
BATTERIES

SUNDAY JANUARY 25, 1998
SUPER
XXXII
BOWL
SAN DIEGO CALIFORNIA

Rich Clarkson

ALL AMERICA'S

EYES (AND CAMERAS)

TURNED TOWARD . . .

David Gonzales

. . . along with the eyes of the Broncos',
coaches in the overhead booth, who
relayed directions to player Ed McCaffrey
on the bench.

Coach Shanahan (above) stayed zeroed in on the task at hand.

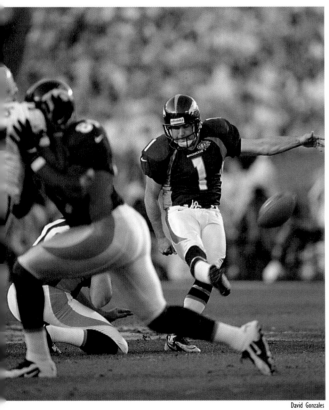

Kicker Jason Elam (above) and punter Tom Rouen (right) pinned the Packers deep in their own territory all evening long.

ELAM'S 51 YARD FIELD GOAL.

IT WAS THE SECOND LONGEST

IN SUPER BOWL HISTORY

AND EXTENDED THE

BRONCOS' LEAD TO 17-7.

Eric Lars Bakke

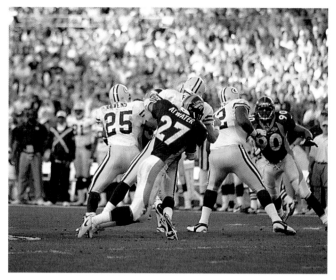

THE DENVER DEFENSE

WAS HITTING EVERY-

THING IN A GREEN AND

GOLD UNIFORM.

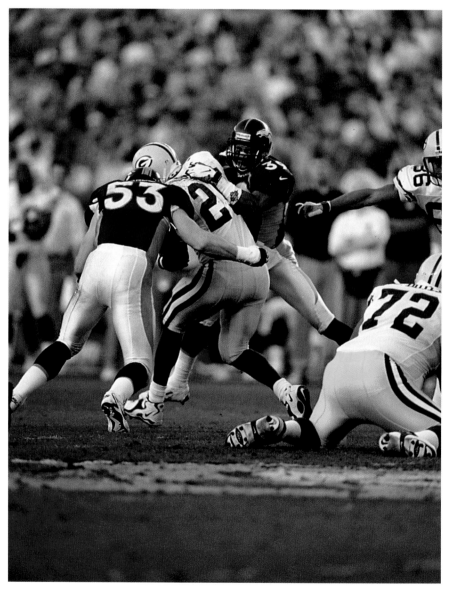

*A Broncos sandwich—
Bill Romanowski and Ray
Crockett slow the Packers.*

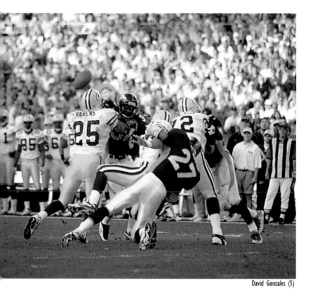

In sequence, Steve Atwater breaks through to throw Packers quarterback Brett Favre to the ground and force the game's second turnover.

The collision of the game came with only 32 seconds left and it resulted in Green Bay having to use their final timeout to attend to receiver Robert Brooks, knocked momentarily unconscious along with Broncos Darrius Johnson and Steve Atwater. With little time and no timeouts left, the game's outcome became more certain.

Ryan McK

Eric Lars Bakke

TO THE FOLKLORE

OF THE BRONCOS,

"THE DIVE" HAS BEEN

ADDED TO "THE DRIVE."

David Gonzales

It was late in the third quarter and it was third down. The score was tied at 17 and the game was undecided. With his receivers covered, Elway kept the ball hurdling into and through three defenders. First down, Denver Broncos. Center Tom Nalen later said, "It motivated us. He was giving it up for the team. We were tired, but when we saw that, we were giving each other high fives and head butts." The Broncos went on to score on the drive and NFL Films had its highlight clip of the game.

EVERY BRONCO

SHARED IN THE GLORY

OF A MOMENT TO

WHICH THEY HAD ALL

CONTRIBUTED.

Whether with clenched fists or open palms, Alfred Williams (far left), Derek Loville (near left) and Tyrone Braxton (below left) all showed what it felt like to be Super Bowl champions.

Rich Clarkson

At midfield for the trophy presentation, Elway first held the Super Bowl trophy aloft, then later showed it in the locker room before a packed meeting with sportswriters in the media tent.

13 YEARS OF NFC
DOMINATION ENDED IN
SAN DIEGO THANKS IN
LARGE PART TO THE
LEGS OF HOMETOWN
HERO TERRELL DAVIS.

David Gonzales

David Gonzales

After the game, the Broncos locker room became the joyous Headquarters of Congratulation with Mike Shanahan hugging John Elway

...then, cornerback Tim McKyer

...and wide receiver Willie Green

Eric Lars Bakke

Anthony Lynn and nine-year old son D'Anton were able to signal "We're number one" when they actually were.

THE SENTIMENTAL FAVORITE OF AN ENTIRE NATION, ELWAY FINALLY RECEIVED HIS LONG-AWAITED MOMENT IN THE SUN

For Elway, the memorable exit from the field with game ball firmly under control was slow as cameramen surrounded his procession. At this moment, there was no hurry for it was a time to savor.

. . . and guard
Mark Schlereth

. . . and Elway with father Jack

. . . and David Diaz-Infante and friend

. . . and Shanahan with wide
receiver Rod Smith.

WE WON WHAT?

By Rick Reilly

Rich Clarkson (3)

Spectators' expressions summed up the Broncos' performance in four previous trips to the big game.

T hey don't understand. This changes everything. *Losing was our identity.* It's like a guy who wakes up to find somebody has replaced his wife with Heather Locklear. We have no idea how to act. After 38 years of watching the Broncos, we'd started to *depend* on losing. You know how cows in the Scottish Highlands fall over when the wind finally stops blowing? That's us.

Denver has never been treated this way by a Super Bowl before. Super Bowls have spit in our soup and dumped it over our heads: 20-10, 39-20, 42-10, 55-10. In the week leading up to this game, the thought of going to another Super Bowl party gave many of us facial tics. Before the playoffs last year, Janet Elway, John's wife, said, "If we're going to get to the Super Bowl and lose, I'd rather we just lose now." Broncos fans understood. It got so bad that we started coping by mocking ourselves. We'd blurt out Broncos jokes just to beat people to the punch line. We repainted highway signs to read I-70, BRONCOS 10.

You know how those people always close the door when the guy tells them they just won $10 million in a publishing house sweepstakes? That's Broncos fans right now. I saw a guy at the post-Super Bowl madhouse downtown with a Samoyed dyed blue and orange and a sign that said WE DID WHAT? We just won Best Actress, and we have no speech prepared. It's crazy. Even the guys we *beat* seemed fairly pleased with the whole situation. "I'm happy for John," said Brett Favre after the game. Hell, Mike Holmgren told his players to *let* Denver score the winning touchdown.

Losing is what glued us to the Broncos. Losing is all we had. Since 1960 we've been addicted to a team that wore striped socks, starred a guy named Floyd and had an unshaved fat man in a barrel for a mascot. But we set a record for sellouts, through blizzard and blowout, because the Broncos were like us — the unloved, the unknown, the underdogs.

See, we knew we were a great city with friendly people and gorgeous views, but we had more insecurities than the National Hair Weave Convention. We constantly have to hear, "Catch *Monday Night Football* tonight at nine Eastern, eight Central and six Pacific." When do *we* watch, during leap years? A CBS newsman once said, "The only thing Denver is Number 1 in is carbon monoxide levels." That kind of thing *forms* you, man.

We did backflips trying to prove we weren't a cow town. We'd sit at our fancy skyscrapers, and yet we figured our visitor sitting across from us was thinking, *Bet she's got a spittoon under there.* We'd flock to any new restaurant that featured waiters with fake accents and $22 entrees just to show we were more than a town that invented the cheeseburger. So what happens when the Summit of Eight arrives? The world leaders go to a restaurant called The Fort and eat buffalo testicles.

But that's all toast now. Therapists by the hundreds are suddenly out of work. The designated dumpsters of the Super Bowl are world champions. We're just going to have to live with it.

Don't blame yourselves, Denver. There's nothing you could have done about it. The fates weren't going to allow the Broncos to lose. How else do you explain the sunrise on Super Bowl morning in San Diego, a brilliant orange and blue? The game being held in the stadium where Denver has its most road wins? The Blue Angels mistiming their entrance and flying over at the *exact* moment Elway is introduced? Terrell Davis spotting the Packers a migraine, a quarter and, for a while, *vision,* and still ending up Super Bowl MVP? Telling you, this thing was fixed by Zeus.

"There's only so many times you can get hit in the forehead with a fist," Elways screamed to a scant 650,000 at the celebratory parade. "This time, we did the punchin'!" It'll take some doing, but we can get used to feeling this good. We can face up the fact that people *like* us, *like* our city, *like* our monster economy, *like* our achingly blue skies, and aren't just being nice to us so we'll give them good directions to Aspen.

Rick Reilly is the senior writer and columnist for Sports Illustrated who has lived in Denver most of his life having covered, watched and agonized with the Broncos for an entire career. He has been named five times Sportswriter of the Year by the National Sportscasters and Sportswriters Association.

Ryan McKee (3)

IT'LL TAKE SOME

DOING, BUT WE CAN

GET USED TO FEELING

THIS GOOD.

The celebration began Sunday night in LoDo as celebrating fans roamed the streets. But the next day began the real celebration.

The triumphant return to Denver came Monday night and to no more fitting place than Mile High Stadium where 40,000 fans waited four chilly hours to welcome the Broncos home with their Super Bowl trophy. Some had arrived at 6:30 A.M. to be at the head of the line when the stadium gates opened.

When the team arrived with owner Pat Bowlen and coach Mike Shanahan in the lead, the crowd cheered wildly. Bowlen walked the Vince Lombardi trophy down the fence for fans to feel the actual prize.

Jennifer Logan

Moments later, John Elway told the crowd, "For 38 years, you guys have been there more than anyone. Isn't it fun to stick your finger in the the air and say you're the best!"

Tight end Shannon Sharpe proclaimed, "We have the best fans in the world and now we have the best football team in the world. Enjoy this, guys."

"This is incredible," cornerback Ray Crockett said looking at the crowd. "I'm at a loss for words, really. I can't explain what I'm feeling right now."

And in the background, Mile High's sound system played the Bruce Springsteen recording, "Born in the USA."

Broncomaniacs filled Mile High Stadium to welcome their conquering heroes home from San Diego. Neil Smith, Mike Shanahan, Shannon Sharpe and John Elway (from left) each took turns thanking the assembled fans.

PAT BOWLEN SHARED WITH THE FANS THE SYMBOL

OF THE BRONCOS' ULTIMATE SUCCESS—THE VINCE

LOMBARDI TROPHY.

Eric Lars Bakke

Ryan McKee (4)

David Gonzales

Broncos fans expressed their appreciation for the team's accomplishment from every conceivable vantage point—some in a more sacrilegious fashion than others.

Eric Lars Bakke

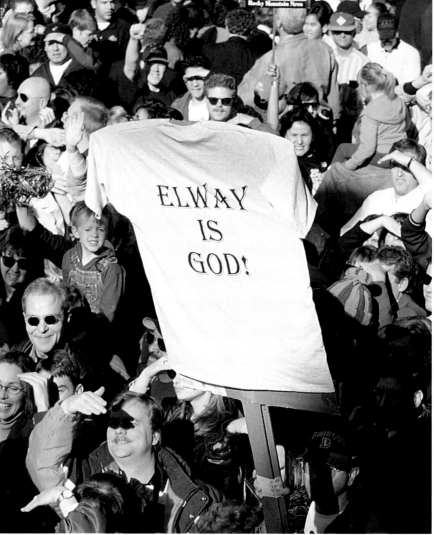

ELWAY
IS
GOD!

Eric Lars Bakke

THE ENTIRE ELWAY

FAMILY WAS ON HAND

TO ENJOY THE VICTORY

PARADE THROUGH

DOWNTOWN DENVER.

Eric Lars Bakke

THE CARAVAN TOOK

NEARLY THREE HOURS

TO TRAVEL ALONG ITS

18-BLOCK ROUTE, AS

650,000 FANS

STRAINED TO GET A

GLIMPSE OF THEIR

BELOVED BRONCOS.

132

For the players, the parade was an opportunity to see firsthand the effect they had on an entire city.

Good seats were hard to find at the rally at the City & County Building.

Eric Lars Bakke

David Gonzales

The rally evoked a rare smile from head coach Mike Shanahan (above).

JOHN ELWAY BLVD

COLORADO GOVERNOR ROY ROMER AND

DENVER MAYOR WELLINGTON WEBB EXTENDED

THE THANKS OF NOT JUST THE CITY, BUT THE

ENTIRE STATE.

David Gonzales

THE SIGHT OF

650,000 BRONCOS

FANS WAS A BIT OVER-

WHELMING—EVEN FOR

THE ELWAY FAMILY.

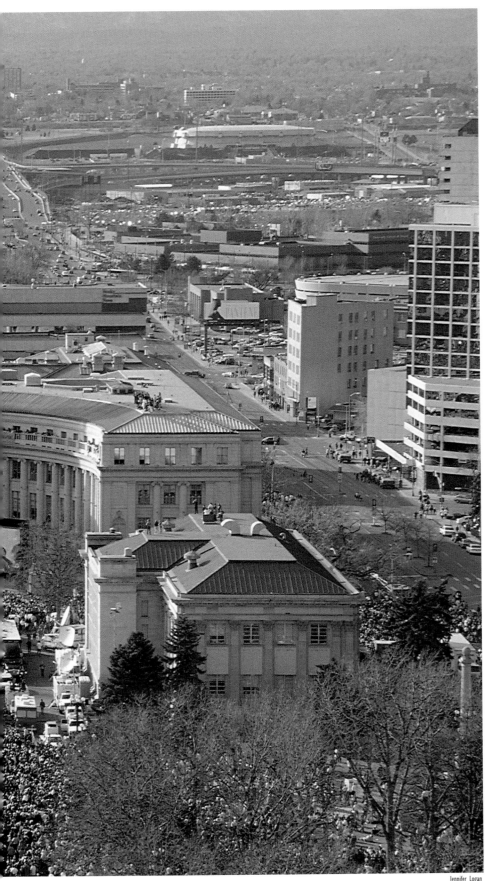

The Rocky Mountains provided the perfect backdrop for the largest public gathering in Colorado history.

VISION
AND
VICTORY

Rod Hanna

1984 marked the beginning of the most successful era in Broncos history—the Pat Bowlen era.

By Pat Bowlen

There are times when people write and say a lot of things that they somehow believe are my opinions about our city and our team. Sometimes those perceptions are accurate, but many times they are way off the mark. This seems to be a good place and time to express my own thoughts about the Denver Broncos, our city and the Super Bowl win that we all shared together.

The way I see it, the 14 seasons in which I have operated the Denver Broncos represent a transition to the modern era of pro football in Denver. When we played in two Super Bowls during the 1980s—and lost those games—we never really got over that. Even though we moved forward as an organization and made it all the way to the big one, those losses didn't leave us. You don't get credit for having made it to the Super Bowl; people only remember the ones who come home with the trophy. As a team and as a city, we were still branded as Super Bowl losers. Those years, we didn't win the big one. John Elway didn't win the big one. I never doubted that we would someday win a Super Bowl. The question in my mind was always how many Super Bowls we would win. With the previous losses, we all wondered how many more chances we would have. I knew there would be other chances.

Now that we're World Champions, there's a difference in the way people view our team, our city and our fans. Fans, other people around the league and other owners look at Denver as a first-class organization, and that's very flattering to us all. Now, those four Super Bowl losses are viewed in a different light—like revisionist history over the course of time. Perhaps they were necessary catalysts behind some of the changes we've made over the years.

Denver has a most unique situation in all of sports. There is an undeniable feeling that exists toward the Broncos that's different from the relationships most other cities have with their teams. The history of the Denver Broncos has always been about the fans—it hasn't been about the ownership. This dates back to the 1960s. Historically, when I look back 24 years before I got here, this franchise really is a remarkable story. During the '60s and early '70s, the team was perceived as one at the bottom of the league. But the fans were still there. Broncos games started to sell out at the start of the '70s, and have done so ever since. There aren't any franchises besides the Washington Redskins and us who can say that. That is a tribute to the city, the fans and the Broncos. In different cities that may not be the case, but here, it is all about the fans. Without the fans, you really don't have a chance.

Everywhere I go people talk about fan support in other cities. But it's hard for me to say that there's another city with the same passion for their football team as we have here in Denver. You can talk about the 49ers, Cowboys or most others, and their fans are different. The support of our fans is not only all-important—it is also legendary. It's a unique situation here, and we are fortunate to have that love and devotion. It's reminiscent in a way of a college-type atmosphere. That special symbiotic situation doesn't reflect the typical image of a sterile professional franchise simply providing one-sided entertainment for the city. It's a lot more than that. Now that we've won the big

THE SUPPORT OF OUR FANS IS NOT ONLY ALL-IMPORTANT—IT IS ALSO LEGENDARY.

Ryan McKee

Bowlen's first stop after returning from San Diego was Mile High Stadium to greet the fans.

Eric Lars Bakke

Bowlen has had only one starting quarterback during his years with the team—John Elway.

one, the fans have tasted victory and their appetites have increased. We've evolved to a higher level. Fans expect more from us and I intend to see that they get it.

There are so many examples of passion and emotion expressed by our fans on a personal level. At the premier of our 1997 season highlight film, for example, we had people from all walks of life coming up to me and expressing heartfelt emotions. Another moment that sticks in my mind came last Thanksgiving when we were helping Daddy Bruce by giving out turkeys and talking with people who were quite disadvantaged. As one talked with people waiting in line, it was clear that they weren't worried about such things as paying a penny on every ten bucks, for example, or organizing political attacks against their football team. These people are die-hard Broncos fans, and even though they don't make it to games they watch on television. Their comments were "Hey, keep it up! Great work! You guys have done great. We love you!" Those comments were sincere, not manufactured. On certain socioeconomic levels, people have nothing to lose—or gain, for that matter—by speaking their minds, and you can depend on blatant sincerity from them.

One is humbled to just be a part of this great relationship between city and team. It's evident throughout the community every day. It doesn't matter whether it's a small gathering or large crowd: you could talk about a parade that has nearly three-quarters-of-a-million people turning out, or 10 to 15 people coming up to shake my hand at a small event. It's remarkable to me. Not only are they the hard-core Broncos fans, but we often don't realize how representative those fans are of the general populace. We have hard-core fans here.

Any team and city that can share that type of love affair can count themselves lucky, and that's why we are so fortunate to be living in Denver.

I read the papers every day, and, unfortunately, what the papers write is not necessarily the absolute reflection of what the fans think. Editors can pick and choose what is printed and what will sell the most papers. People generally are not shy about approaching me with their thoughts, and I think comments expressed in person by our fans are a really good barometer of what's going on out there. Fans are out there and they speak in one voice—a loud one. A lot of times, those writing stories in the press do not reflect that voice.

Winning the World Championship really exonerated every Broncos fan everywhere who had to put up with the attitude of, "Yeah, you guys are a good team, and John Elway might be a great quarterback . . . but you never won the big one." Immediately after the Super Bowl, we went to New York for ESPN's ESPY Awards, at which time the Broncos received the Team of the Year and Game of the Year honors. One of the most surprising things to me was the reaction of New Yorkers. New Yorkers are renowned for their chilly, "who cares" attitude, and they seem to like it that way. I've spent a lot of time in New York. But this time, everywhere I went, nearly every cab driver, every doorman and every street vendor said "Boy, are we happy you won! Great game, great for John, great for you!" I'm talking about New York City here—not Denver, Colorado. That kind of response is very gratifying to every Broncos fan and member of the organization.

The more I reflected prior to the Super Bowl, the more I realized that winning the game would be an exclamation point on John's career. That's why I said "This one's for John!" when the game was over. Winning is what it was all about, and it wasn't possible to separate John from the equation of Denver and the Broncos. John and the Denver Broncos are an entity. Even people from other cities who weren't necessarily pulling for us were pulling for John. That whole scenario ties directly to the community, because fans have true emotional ownership in the team and John's career.

The Lombardi Trophy itself has been a huge access thing. I joke when I say it would make me a lot more popular if I could take it with me everywhere. It's not a joke; it's the truth! It's so amazing to me how people just want to touch it, be a part of it. People sometimes are so awed, so overwhelmed by it, they ask if it's the real trophy. It's like we all worked so hard to win it and now that we have it, it belongs to the entire community, as well as the organization. It's a real symbol.

Let me explain something about the essence of ownership of professional sports teams. If you want to be involved for the money, as in an ordinary business, pro sports is not the place to be. You are in it for the excitement of being involved. Competition is in your blood, and the gauge of your success is called winning. Owners don't get big contracts. If they make money, they turn around and sink it right back into the organi-

zation. Why? Because they want to win. Winning the World Championship is the ultimate goal. Yes, you get a lot of personal satisfaction out of that. That's why you go to work every day. Winning is what you are really trying to do. If you're looking at the bottom line—like I just said—you're in the wrong business. What you ought to be looking at are the win and loss columns. That is what people will forever judge me on, and I expect that when they put me in my grave the epitaph will read "He won four Super Bowls; he was a great owner," or "He didn't win any; he was a lousy owner."

That's what I believe, and winning championships is the only goal this organization will ever have.

ONE IS HUMBLED TO JUST BE A PART OF THIS GREAT RELATIONSHIP BETWEEN CITY AND TEAM.

Ryan McKee

Bowlen's vision should ensure the franchise's success for years to come.

The traditional White House salute to the world champions took place in June when President Clinton welcomed the Broncos to the East Room for a relaxed visit with the players, Mike Shanahan and Pat Bowlen. The team flew to Washington for a whirlwind day that included time with the Colorado Congressional delegation, a luncheon and VIP tour of the White House.

The president, himself a football fan, told the team, "Maybe the most remarkable thing was the loyalty of the community and the steadfastness of John Elway."

Bowlen got the day's biggest laugh and applause when he told the president, "I was told you were a fan of the Broncos and were rooting for us—and I believe you."

Arriving at the White House, the team was escorted down the hallway that connects the west wing to the East Room.

Players were surprised at how knowledgeable the president was about the team.

A string ensemble from the Marine Corps band played in the foyer after the ceremonies.

Glenn Cadrez (above) rested for a moment after the White House tour beneath an oil painting of John F. Kennedy.

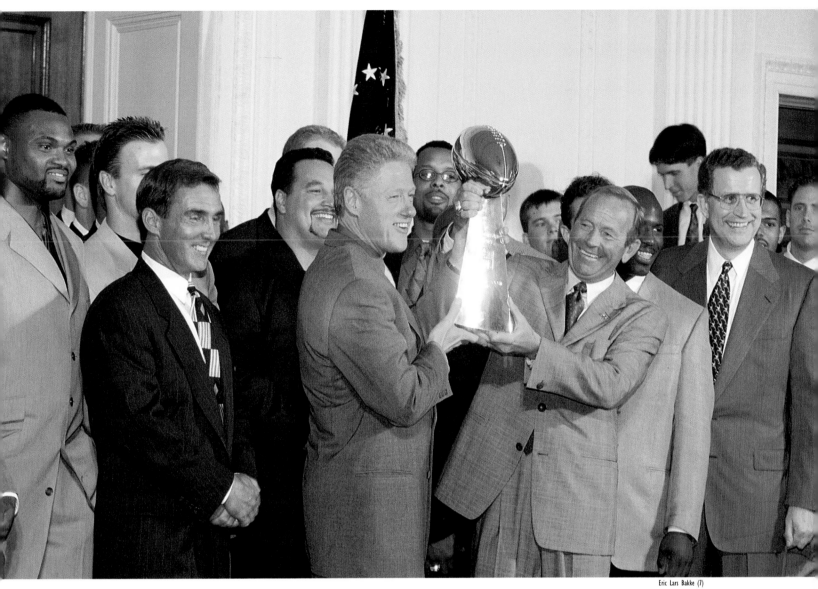

Pat Bowlen and President Clinton lifted the Super Bowl trophy high as Mike Shanahan and NFL Commissioner Paul Tagliabue enjoyed the moment.

David Diaz-Infante and the president stood back to back to settle the discussion as to who was taller.

The president and Rod Smith—one of three native Arkansans on the Broncos—shared talk of their native state.

THE PHOTOGRAPHERS

ERIC LARS BAKKE was the Broncos' team photographer from 1989 to the present. He has worked on newspapers in Idaho, Kansas and was formerly chief photographer of the *Denver Post.* Now a freelance photographer, his work has appeared in many magazines, including *Sports Illustrated.* He lives in Evergreen.

ROD HANNA was the team photographer for the Broncos from 1979–89 after serving in a similar capacity for the Kansas City Chiefs. An Iowa native, he was among a handful of photographers to cover many NFL championship games, including Super Bowl I. Today, he is vice president of marketing for the Steamboat Ski & Resort Corporation and lives in Steamboat Springs.

DAVID GONZALES is a staff photographer and project manager for Rich Clarkson and Associates covering the Broncos, the Colorado Rockies and NCAA championships regularly. He is a graduate of Stanford University and now lives in Denver.

RYAN McKEE is a California native who joined the staff of Rich Clarkson and Associates in 1997 and is a Fresno State University journalism graduate. As staff photographer and project manager, he covered the Broncos regularly and lives in Denver.

RICH CLARKSON is the founder of the group that now creates all photography and imaging for the Denver Broncos. Formerly director of photography of *National Geographic* magazine, he started his company in Denver ten years ago. In addition to heading the photo department of the *Topeka (Ks.) Capital-Journal* and as assistant managing editor of *The Denver Post*, he has been a longtime *Sports Illustrated* contributing photographer, with more than 60 covers to his credit. For *Time* and *Sports Illustrated* magazines, he has covered seven summer Olympics, including serving as director of photography for the Olympic Stadium in 1996 at Atlanta. He lives in Denver.

David Gonzales

ACKNOWLEDGMENTS

While the many Denver and Colorado sportswriters who covered the Broncos Super Bowl season wrote incisively and thoroughly during the season, we tried to add to the championship story by including the thoughts of some individuals not regularly heard nor read by Broncos fans.

Those essayists all expressed their pleasure in being asked to contribute and all gave special attention to their parts. Doug Looney was particularly valuable in working with some of these individuals, getting their exact thoughts into the final form. Our special thanks go to those individuals for their contributions.

Steve Harbula from the Broncos was the team's primary contributor to the book's content. Jim Saccomano, Sara Gilbertson and Paul Kirk were extremely helpful in bringing forward the team's archives and records and in obtaining the cooperation of staff and players. Thanks also go to Pat Bowlen, John Beake, Mike Shanahan and David Wass for the support and guidance they provide every day to the entire Broncos organization.

While we wanted to credit all photographers, many photographs from the archives were unfortunately filed anonymously and we were unable to do so. Special help also came from Janet Reeves of *The Rocky Mountain News* and John Sunderland of *The Denver Post* and we thank them.

And certainly the coordination of Emmett Jordan, the help of Jennifer Logan and Rick Garber along with the design expertise of Carrie Jordan were instrumental in the production of the book.

GAMEDAY

BRONCOS vs. BROWNS

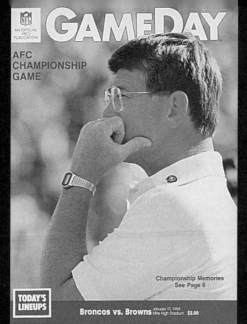

GAMEDAY

AN OFFICIAL PRO! PUBLICATION

AFC CHAMPIONSHIP GAME

Championship Memories
See Page 6

TODAY'S LINEUPS

Broncos vs. Browns January 17, 1988 Mile High Stadium $2.00

pro!

THE OFFICIAL MAGAZINE OF THE NATIONAL

49ERS EDITION

The Denver Broncos

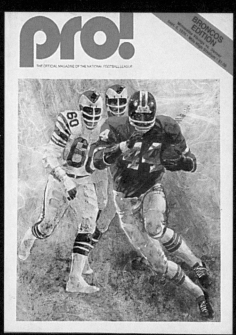

pro!

THE OFFICIAL MAGAZINE OF THE NATIONAL FOOTBALL LEAGUE

BRONCOS EDITION

NFL GAMEDAY

Dennis Smith #49   Steve Atwater #27

LAST LINE OF DEFENSE

BRONCOS vs. SEAHAWKS $3.00

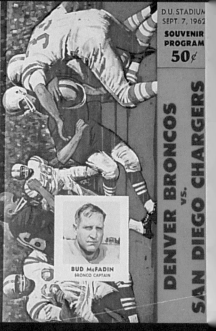

D.U. STADIUM SEPT. 7, 1962

SOUVENIR PROGRAM 50¢

DENVER BRONCOS vs. SAN DIEGO CHARGERS

BUD McFADIN
BRONCO CAPTAIN

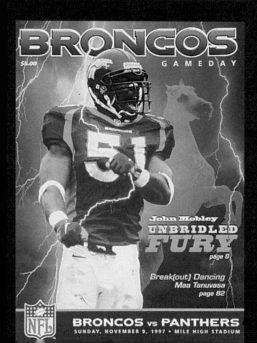

BRONCOS
GAMEDAY

$5.00

John Mobley
UNBRIDLED FURY
page 8

Break(out) Dancing
Maa Tanuvasa
page 82

BRONCOS vs PANTHERS
SUNDAY, NOVEMBER 9, 1997 • MILE HIGH STADIUM

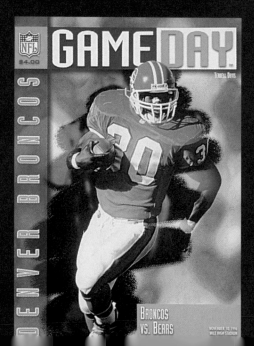

GAMEDAY

$4.00

DENVER BRONCOS

BRONCOS vs. BEARS
NOVEMBER 10, 1996
MILE HIGH STADIUM

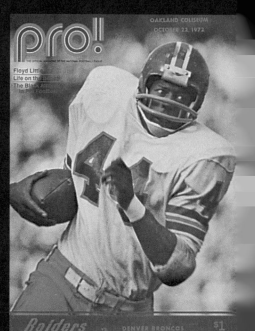

pro!

OAKLAND COLISEUM
OCTOBER 22, 1972

Floyd Little
Life on the Edge
The Black All...

Raiders   vs. DENVER BRONCOS $1